Cynthia Rose was born in Texas. She has lived and worked in London since 1975. She worked on the *London Daily News*, was deputy editor of *Wire* jazz magazine and editor of the London arts weekly *City Limits*. Her broadcasting work includes *The Late Show, Behind the Headlines* and *Start the Week*. *Living in America* is her first book.

LIVING IN AMERICA

the soul saga of james brown

Cynthia Rose

SERPENT'S
TAIL

British Library Cataloguing in Publication Data

Rose, Cynthia

　Living in America: the soul saga of James Brown.

　1. Soul music. Brown, James, 1928 –

　I. Title

　782.421644092

ISBN 1-85242-209-2

Every effort has been made to locate the copyright owners of the material quoted in the text. Omissions brought to our attention will be credited in subsequent printings. Grateful acknowledgement is made to the following publishers: Intersong Music Ltd (for "Please Please Please", "Money Won't Change You", "Licking Stick", "I Don't Want Nobody To Give Me Nothin' [Open Up The Door, I'll Get It Myself]", "Hell", "Funky President", "I'll Go Crazy", "The Soul Of A Black Man", "The Payback", "Let A Man Come In and Do The Popcorn, Parts 1 & 2" by James Brown); Island Music Publishing (for "Don't Believe The Hype" by Public Enemy); and Songwriter Services (for "Express Yourself" by NWA).

This edition first published 1990 by

Serpent's Tail, 4 Blackstock Mews, London N4

Set in 9½/14pt Garamond by AKM Associates (UK) Ltd, London

Printed on acid-free paper by

Nørhaven A/S, Viborg Denmark

contents

Acknowledgements

It would have been impossible to start or complete this project without speaking to James Brown himself – for the time he took, under extraordinary circumstances, many thanks, Mr Brown. Thanks also to Mr William H Glenn, President of James Brown Enterprises. Two other people deserve profound thanks for their extraordinary support: Matthew Best and Dr Paul Gilroy.

My gratitude to Cliff White, whose stalwart labours have brought so much of James Brown to so many people, to London's Cornflake Shop for the use of their fine fine stereo, to Francis Archibald of South Carolina's State Park Correctional Center, and especially to: Vicki Anderson, Bobby Byrd, Alfred "Pee Wee" Ellis, Maceo Parker, Fred Wesley, Haji Akhba, Robert Farris Thompson, Tom and Dora Joyner, Afrika Bambaataa, Gerri Hirshey, Beresford Romeo, Linton Kwesi Johnson, Angus Wynne III, Susie Slack, Susan Hankla, Trevor "Madhatter" Nelson, Norman Jay, Steve Jerviere, The Wikki Wikki Nippy Jones, Dave V-J and Max L-X, Tim Westwood, Catherine Acquah, Polly and William Hootkins, Laney Yarber and Joe Flaten, Cat Ledger, Sumter Bruton, Christina Patoski and Lindy Barger, Cynthia Leu, Michael Weldon, Tony Farsides, Clay McNear, the churches of Evans Avenue, Fort Worth, Gavin Hills, Eric and Tre, David Upshal, Soul II Soul, Sally Holloway, Jeff Liles, Caroline Roux, Linda and Ed Blackburn, Vron Ware, Marcus Joel Gilroy Ware and Cora Gilroy Ware, Jane

Goddard, Christine Donougher and Roderick Conway Morris, Neal Caldwell, The Black Audio Film Collective, DJ Ego and Judge Mental, and the staff at Red Records, Soho, Honest Jon's, Rough Trade Records and VVV Records, Dallas. Thanks for the prayers of Zelma Patrick and to Lloyd "Daddy Bug" Brown – who showed me how to really see a city where I had lived for years.

May James Brown be free. And may Richard "Cartoon" Campbell (1961-1980) and Donald White (1972-1989) continue to live in our hearts, memories, and actions.

For my parents
and
Mr & Mrs C W Beard

"He has no political skills, no diplomacy. However, my mother loves James Brown. He is the most charming person in the world when he needs to be – he could charm the pants off a nun. My mother to this day, asks, "How's Mr Brown? He's just the *nicest* person." And I say to her, mother, you don't know this man like I do.

"Once that charm gets on you, you never lose it. He could beat up an old lady in the street and you could see it happening. But if you been charmed by James Brown you just say: 'She shouldn't have done that to him!' I've seen a lot of women that loved him, loved him just like that. And he'll explain whatever he does. He's bigger than life, broader than the average person."

Fred Wesley, October 1989

"When I do my music, I include a lot of people, but nobody's really involved except myself. Just God and me. I guess I'm like Einstein – let 'em worry about my theory after I'm dead."

James Brown, November, 1989

LIVING IN AMERICA

born at the square root of soul

"The idea of the Negro having 'roots' and that they are a valuable possession, rather than the source of ineradicable shame, is perhaps the profoundest change within the Negro consciousness since the early part of the century."

LeRoi Jones, *Blues People*, 1963

"Black music shows the past," the inmate at South Carolina's State Park Correctional Centre is telling me in gravelly, Biblical tones. "That is soul music, living history. And, right now, there's a question mark hanging over James Brown. I've been stopped, that's what the people are thinking.

"Still," the raspy tones tighten, "I have been stopped before." James J Brown, Jr, pauses, his grip on the prison telephone shifting. His voice is so gruff and lowdown sometimes it threatens to disappear altogether, swallowed by a rich Southern accent. "I was stopped for two years, I was stopped for seven. But I've always been able to express myself and bounce back."

A titan of popular music whose leadership tyrannies constitute a showbiz legend in themselves, James Brown is hardly Uriah Heep. Yet, these days, the man who kick-started funk music *does* seem to be mulling things over. Ten months into serving two concurrent six- year prison sentences (for a two-state automobile chase in 1988 and a series of linked misdemeanours), Brown's mind is clearly back on the one thing his life and career epitomize: African-American survival.

For thirty-three years of public exposure, in conversations, interviews and onstage patter, the singer has always reiterated the touchstones of his personal endurance. Born, in the piney woods of rural South Carolina, to parents who speedily parted. (Brown did not see his mother again until two decades later, when he was already a star.) Raised on cornbread and "salad we picked in the woods" until the tender age of four. Then packed off to an aunt in Georgia: a woman named Handsome and nicknamed "Honey", who bossed an Augusta brothel. A kid who grew up fast in mean streets – dancing, stealing and pimping to live, with nobody really bothered whether he happened to make it or not. A streetwise adolescent sent to prison for eight to sixteen years – three of which he served.

A celebrity who could never outrun, outwit or buy out those central facts, Brown decided, instead, to face them down by invoking his need and hunger and loneliness over and over. And the glory of James Brown's most famous, most unearthly screams resides in the sheer, atomic audacity of that aim.

"Back then," Brown will tell you of his childhood, "I was frightened. I didn't know ANYTHING." Then, as an eerie cackle erupts from the very base of his sandpaper larynx, "But I did know I was *hungry*. I knew I had to eat, I had to get that money."

And get the money he did. Because, at a tender age, Brown picked up on something else. In 1978, music journalist Kristine McKenna asked the performer if, as a child, he had felt destined for stardom. Brown looked her straight in the eye and replied: "I knew one thing – that I was different. Thirty years ago, people would pay ten cents to see me dance because I was different."

A quarter of a century and 114 hit singles later, it's hard to even estimate just *how* different. For Brown became the Andy Warhol of twentieth-century sound: a talent without whom it is simply impossible to try and imagine modern popular music. Mention his name and a litany of classics comes cascading down through the years: "Please, Please, Please", "Papa's Got A Brand New Bag", "Out of Sight", "I Feel Good (I Got You)", "Get Up, I Feel Like Being A Sex Machine", "Night Train", "It's A Man's Man's Man's World", "Cold Sweat", "Say It Loud, I'm Black And I'm Proud", "Give It Up Or Turnit a Loose", "I Don't Want Nobody To Give Me Nothing", "King Heroin", "Get On The Good Foot", "The Payback", "Living In America", "I'm Real". The dime-a-dance shindigs of his childhood gave birth to international permutations:

the slop, boogaloo, Popcorn, robot and goodfoot – steps since assimilated by pop superstars like Mick Jagger, Prince, Michael Jackson. And Brown has recorded more hit records than Aretha Franklin, Ray Charles, U2, Bruce Springsteen or Michael Jackson.

James Brown has sat in audience with African potentates, US Presidents and a pope. He has campaigned with Black Power heavies, calmed race riots, toured to Vietnam and Mother Africa. He is the source – twenty years apart – of two American musical genres: funk and hip-hop or "rap". In the 1960s, Brown's ego built the biggest, baddest stage show America had ever seen, and captured it live on vinyl to yield a landmark, million-selling album (*The James Brown Show Live At The Apollo* in October, 1962). Then he piloted it straight where soul had never gone – into the parlour of Uncle Sam's snow-white middle class.

A wild and churning turbine of an ensemble – but one which functioned with constant rehearsal and military precision – his James Brown Revue sliced up and down the US like a chainsaw from the early '60s through the mid'70s. Shaking and shimmying, spinning and pirouetting across any stage he could commandeer, its frontman became the cynosure of every eye in every house. Brown was determined to stamp his personality on black America above and beyond its awareness of his contemporary rivals – men like Ray Charles, Sam Cooke, Little Richard, Jackie Wilson and Otis Redding – to make himself Living History. And to accomplish that he worked triple-time using everything he could find.

"Thing about it is," he now says proudly, "I always *doubled myself*. Whatever it was, I tried for twice over."

This was more than just energy – it was pure cultural confidence. James Brown wasn't some preacher who urged black America to work (or wait) for a brighter day. Nor was he a showbiz charlatan who hustled them up the illusion of liberation, only to watch it melt away with the bright house lights or the dawn. No – James Brown was *on the one*. He was the RIGHT-NOW black man, who embraced everything his colour could betoken. Including, as Amiri Baraka (then LeRoi Jones) put it in 1963, the attendant muses of "self-division, self-hatred, stoicism and, finally, quixotic optimism".

Brown's specific recipe inspired awe in contemporary be-holders, who ranged from Elvis and Little Richard through a diminutive Michael Jackson. The King of the One Nighters, as he became known by the 1960s, was lauded in album liner notes and *Jet* magazine write-ups which rivalled even his fervent fans (and that was saying a lot).

"During any thirty-day period," gushed the copy on 1964's *Pure Dynamite* sleeve, "James Brown will give away over 5,000 pictures; make gifts of 1,000 pairs of cuff links to some of his lucky fans; wear 120 freshly laundered suits; change uniforms over 150 times; wear more than 30 pairs of shoes; perform over 4,800 minutes on stage and the bandstand; sing and play over 960 songs; play more shows and dances than any other singer or musician active in the business today; lose up to 7 pounds each performance; write several new songs; prepare for his next recording session; pose for publicity pictures; visit DJs in radio stations and, in his spare time, try to get enough sleep to please his personal physician." (Statistics courtesy of Leon Fisher, *Open Mike* magazine.) What the expansive Fisher failed to note was that Brown also literally plotted his own trajectory, hassling and conferring with road managers in hotel rooms or on the phone, road maps fanned out around him on the floor. At the height of his popularity, Brown controlled the investment of almost every dollar he earned. The suitcases he carried bulged with hundreds of thousands in cash and, after 1965, with his jealously-guarded master tapes.

But such statistics can measure only a fraction of James Brown's story. The latest in black America's slang, locomotion, romantic come-ons, coiffures and tailoring – Brown went after them all, corralling daily fads and fashions into his personal stock of histrionic stage voodoo. Take, for instance, the suitcase prop of solicitor George Haines, a flamboyant white prosecutor who sent 16-year-old James to jail in 1949 ("Your Honour, here's my suitcase! If you let this man go free, I'll pack up and FLEE this town!"). That suitcase became a signature in the paroled entertainer's late 1950s show: a red prop emblazoned on one side with *Please, Please, Please* and on the other with *Baby, Take My Hand.* Brown would use it to close a set – collapsing and being helped offstage by one or two of his Famous Flames: backing-singers who would throw a coat around his shoulders, then make as if to support him. Audience approval, of course, would then "imprison" Brown once more, calling him back for numerous frantic encores.

This dramatic exercise was already well-known to both the singer and his black audience from the rousing "Soul Jerker" preachers of the Baptist South. And it produced Brown's most notorious trademark: the ritualistic "cape routine". Explained in print a hundred times, decoded by sociologists and semiologists as well as music critics, this finale was enshrined on film in 1965's famous *The TAMI Show.* In Rolling Stone's *The History of Rock and Roll,* critic Robert Palmer describes Brown's usual procedure thus:

As he wrenched out the pleading refrain to "Please, Please, Please", he would sink slowly to his knees, writhing . . . until finally, still singing, he collapsed in a heap. Famous Flames Bobby Bennett and Lloyd Stallworth would approach him hesitantly. One would produce a purple cape and, reverently draping it over the fallen singer's body, help him to his feet and slowly escort him offstage. Brown, still holding the microphone, would begin to drag his feet, struggle, and after a dramatic pause, shake off the cape and walk deliberately back to the stage centre. There he would lurch into another chorus only to drop to his knees again, his voice a hoarse sob. The routine was repeated, this time with a gold cape. Once again Brown waited until the last minute, shook off his attendants, returned to the front of the stage, began singing, feigned collapse. Finally, a jet black cape was produced and Brown and the Flames left the stage while the band played on. The audiences, absolutely spent . . . would shout themselves hoarse for more, wondering all the while how Brown could possibly top what he'd already done. And then Mr Dynamite would appear, wearing a new suit, a prop suitcase in his hand, propelling himself across the stage on one foot, thumb out as if hitching a ride to the next town.

"That *TAMI Show* was the highest energy thing has ever *been*," says Brown twenty-four years after his most famous filmed appearance. "I danced so hard that my manager cried. But I really *had to*. What I was up against was pop artists – and I was R'n'B. I had to show 'em the difference, and, believe me, it was hard." (Though most remembered today for Brown's all-out humiliation of a then-ascendant Mick Jagger, the surprisingly broad-based

TAMI Show also included Marvin Gaye, Jan and Dean, the Beach Boys, Smokey Robinson and the Miracles and the Supremes.)

Through his complete concentration onstage, his seemingly desperate conviction and his mighty set of lungs, James Brown could achieve an apotheosis capable of satisfying the most hallucinatory Baptist. He even managed to transcend those demons of self against which, at bottom, his battle has always been pitched. But Brown transcended them only on the stage.

As his career expanded, more and more colleagues came to resent the flip side of his singular talent: the paranoia, the inventive forms of emotional manipulation he practised on employees, his cavalier treatment of women.

And for years, unsavoury rumours made the rounds: James, they alleged, beat both wives and girlfriends, including songstress Tammi Terrell, who died in 1970 after collapsing onstage in the arms of later singing partner Marvin Gaye. *James* took all the credit for the compositional triumphs of many associates. *James* enslaved his retinue by claiming that, if they left him, he'd see that they never worked again. During his second, late '80s, spell in prison, many of Brown's most well-known ex-employees have underscored his three decades of creativity with horror stories of financial extortion, woman-beating and – latterly – drug abuse. Others, of equally venerable attachment to the singer, still refuse to hear or utter a single word against him.

"James was bossy and paranoid," says trombone player Fred Wesley, whose career with Brown lasted seven years, many spent as the band's influential arranger. "I didn't see why someone of his stature would be so defensive. I couldn't understand the way he treated his band, why he was so *evil.* He was JAMES BROWN! Some people would be glad just to touch him. And yet he was jealous of women, jealous of what clothes people wore, jealous of *every little thing*".

"It was ridiculous," says Wesley, "that somebody of his power and popularity could be so insecure. But later on, I got to understand. He had to have been like that, just to stay alive. People that knew him as a kid can tell you – we're talking about a 3-, 4-year-old child who actually didn't live anywhere. Nobody fed him, nobody bathed him. He didn't *have* a place to live. He survived on sheer guts.

"So I got to understand him being so defensive and protective. I didn't like it and I don't ever care to be in his company again. And it doesn't excuse a lot of his actions – but I do understand the man."

Even Brown's sharpest critics, such as songstress Vicki Anderson (wife of Bobby Byrd, the Famous Flame whose mother got Brown paroled from his teenage prison term and took him into her home) will not deny Brown's singularity – or the power it brought him. "I've never truly seen another person like James," says Anderson. "I know he's got a heart, cause he's livin'. He has common sense and he's not retarded. And it's not impossible for him to change, although it's not really likely. But if he *did* change, he would certainly be a very great person. Cause I have seen him play *so* well, be *so* good, that he completely transcends the man he is."

Biblical stuff indeed, the transformation of man through will. But Brown is also consummate showbiz: a century of black vaudeville and theatre distilled and filtered through with a religion that evolved, in the first place, to satisfy Afro-America's innermost needs. Two decades after Brown first breached the US charts, Bruce Springsteen would incorporate a comic version of

Jamesian collapse-and-resurrection into his act. But back in the 1960s, when white suburban teens caught JB on *The TAMI Show* or Dick Clark's *Where the Action Is*, what they saw might just as well have been beamed in from outer space.

Writer Gerri Hirshey who, in 1984's *Nowhere To Run*, would draw pop's sharpest portrait of Brown to date, was twelve when she witnessed this spectacle: a white pre-teen from upper New England. "He came on Ed Sullivan's show," she remembers, "and they just let him rip. That was the first time I saw the cape, and I knew it was wonderful showbiz. But I *believed* him, too. I believed he was really out flat. Then – I believed he was resurrected.

"For a lot of white kids like me," Hirshey speculates, "I think this contained a large element of envy. It was partly a be-cool thing. But, with James, responding extended beyond even that. Because – and this is just what Michael Jackson told me many years later – James just got so out of himself. He could be *exactly* what he wanted. He made no compromise."

In the shadow of Martin Luther King, and with the Black Panthers at his back, Brown took '60s white America very much on his own terms and in his own voice. Unlike the great Sam Cooke, who sang "asked" when he would have said "ax'd". Unlike Ray Charles, who as critic Nik Cohn has put it, "smothered his great natural force in wads of candy floss" after '62. Unlike marvellous Motown, with its explicit dreams of a white clientele, its etiquette classes and corporate grooming tips. No: *James Brown* came screaming into the Eisenhower '50s and Kennedy '60s – straight from the hearts of black America. And it's because of James Brown that a '90s pop star like Bobby Brown can promise the mainstream radio listener he'll "rock *wit'cha* all night long".

Musically, Brown fused rural rhythm and blues (R'n'B) and its big-band swing with "sanctified" gospel: the rhapsodic ecstatic religion of the deepest, blackest South. Where Nat "King" Cole drew the image of the dark man towards traditional sophistication, Brown turned assimilation around. He pulled theatre towards his colour, he used his blackness as a magnet backed with all the force and drama of the charismatic church. Even today, gospel remains James Brown's music of choice – the albums he will play at home and his favourite after-work cool-out therapy.

In Brown's art, gospel is central. But so is a certain fantastic, phantasmagorical southern surrealism. Travelling with him periodically between '78 and '84, Gerri Hirshey observed a primal connection between the two – as well as the invocations each would make to memory. "The weird sort of mystical aspect to James always kind of threw me. The things he would tell me about myself – or then he'd tell you something was going to happen, then later it would. Truly, it was just spooky. Also, he will go off into these strange lectures on other religions. He is very religious, absolutely so. But when he sings gospel after a show, it is always a key to memory. This big, communal churchy thing would be going on . . . then James would go kind of sit off to the side. And, depending upon what town he was in, he would start to reminisce through twenty years of memories in that city."

James and Elvis Presley briefly became what Hirshey calls "gospel pals". Meeting in California circa 1966 (and later in Las Vegas) the two Southern giants shut the door, shut out the world, and harmonized together on familiar chestnuts like "Old Blind Barnabas", jointly invoking a poor, rural South where the communal aspiration was somehow to ascend. Brown says it has always calmed him to sing such "jubilee" – the tightly harmonized, upbeat gospel which trained the popular stars of his youth: the Ravens, Orioles, and Five Royales, with their elegant "doo-wop" styles.

In 1952, gospel even got the embryonic Mr Excitement out of jail. "I met James on the prison baseball field," says his lifelong friend Bobby Byrd – who was a visitor rather than a fellow inmate. "I was playing shortstop and he was at the bat. He was comin' from first to second base and they threw me the ball and James ran right over me. He helped me up and we laughed and started talkin' about our gospel groups." Bobby's Gospel Starlighters were well-known within a sixty-mile radius of tiny Alto, Georgia – where James was serving his time for petty thieving at the Georgia Juvenile Training Institute. Inside, says Byrd, Brown's personal quartet of inmates "had their own gospel platform", and they knew James as "Music Box".

The Byrd-Brown collision was a portent of events to come. Within a fortnight, Bobby's mother had seen the Institute Warden, armed with a church petition containing over 200 names. It asked that young James Brown be released into the care of the local Baptist community. Three years and a day after his arrest, the future Godfather did get sprung – thanks to Mrs Byrd's Mount Zion Baptist Church. And three months later, Brown would desert Bobby's sister's community choir, in order to join Byrd's Gospel Starlighters.

"In those groups then, you had two leaders," says Bobby Byrd today. "So it was me and him, back and forth." But such democracy didn't last long. Staying on top of topical hits – strong, lead-with-harmony-backup pieces by the Keys, the Clovers, the Five Royales — Byrd's group became first the Avons, then the

"Toccoa Band". Under the unforeseen pressure of James Brown's burgeoning drive, they found their style and repertoire subject to constant change and experiment.

They were gigging acapella, for instance, with only their feet and hands for accompaniment: circumstances which made Brown's preternatural lungpower very valuable. But James soon revealed that he possessed an absolute armoury of inventive gimmicks. If a juke joint or club looked unpromising, he would make its proprietor close the curtains or paper over the windows – to pique curiosity and spark envy among the passers-by. And, once a crowd was enticed inside, Brown would grab any prop in the place which might possibly enhance his act. He danced with brooms and dust-mops, made love to fraternity-house furniture, executed baseball slides on any remotely level floor. Generally, says Bobby Byrd, he ran the band personnel ragged with his ceaseless plans and schemes. "But, back in those days James was a great guy. Before he hit, you know, he just *couldn't* do enough for you."

Primed by prison and childhood struggle, James Brown knew how to take care of business. Before prison put an end to his schooling – it took him out of the seventh grade – Brown's own group, the Cremona Trio, had looked very promising. They had won church social prizes and featured on local talent shows. Now, within four years, James managed to hustle Bobby's band – rechristened the Flames and soon devoted to backing Brown's solo self – attention from Ralph Bass, a travelling talent scout. Bass worked for Federal Records, a subsidiary of Cincinatti, Ohio's King label. King was a somewhat old-fashioned outfit founded in 1944 to merchandise blues and hillbilly harmony. But during the 1950s, King would become one of America's most far-ranging independents – combining records by Steve Lawrence with gospel, R'n'B and jazz.

"At first," says Bobby Byrd, "our biggest people for influence were Hank Ballard and the Midnighters, the Clovers, the Five Royales. We wasn't ever all gospel, we was into the popular stuff. But it was certainly gospel that gave us that real high-energy thing."

Then came Little Richard – Georgia's particular local hero. "Little Richard came to Toccoa," says Byrd. "And he told us we could go on at his intermission. That went *real* good, didn't nobody move from their seats. This was when we started really workin' 'Please Please Please'."

Extracted from "Baby Please Don't Go" by R'n'B balladeers the Orioles, "Please Please Please" was a number composed by Brown and Johnny Terry, the Flame with whom James had "sung my way out of prison". Worked up in front of live crowds for two years before it was even laid down as a demo, the tune became James Brown's initial ultra-flamboyant finale.

As voiced by the Famous Flames, the song's repetitive harmonic backdrops ("Please, please – don't go!"/"You done me wrong – you done me wrong!") pointed established doo-wop tradition in the direction of call-and-response antiphony . . . already a common sound in surrounding R'n'B. Upfront, Brown pleads and screams in classic "cry singer" mode – the raw, suggestive, I'll-do-anything style he had absorbed from Southern blues belters like Wynonie Harris and Roy Brown. But, even on the eventual recording of "Please Please Please" (definitely tame compared to '62's subsequent album version on *Live At The Apollo*), a listener can detect the essential James "Butane" Brown being born. It's clear, for instance, that this singer's basic interest is commanded more by the beats than the sentiment, more by the ritual of invocations than by their actual import. Audibly, he relishes every possible chance to twist, transmute and extemporize the *sound* of his vocal pleas.

Drawing on deep-seated expectations within a black audience already schooled by both bluesmen and preachers, "Please" was a viable autograph for Brown's emerging psyche. For several years, in several guises, the number allowed him to test and shape his various talents: vocal stamina, improvisation, superb interpretive dancing and the quirks of a natural stylist. Still, it would be almost three years from that first recording, a regional hit, to the *national* R'n'B charts – which Brown finally reached with "Try Me" (a gospel rewrite) in November of 1958. In between, he had cut *nine* records – all of which failed completely.

Once he started to matter in black America, however, Brown relentlessly pushed himself forward, constantly foregrounding who HE was. Over and over, night after night, year after year, he would formalize and declare his aims with a litany of titles. Each, he hoped, would prove more irresistible to that audience he had set out to bind unto him. And, to the same end, each must be ever more indicative of the significance in his colour. "Mr Please Please Please" became "The Ruler of R'n'B", "King of the One Nighters", "Mister Dynamite Himself", "The Hardest Working Man in Showbusiness", "Mr Excitement", James "Butane" Brown, "Soul Brother No 1", "Mr Superbad", "The Original Disco Man", "Minister of the New New Super Heavy Funk" – THE Godfather of Soul and the Forefather of Hip-Hop.

This multiplicity of names sprang from the same roots as the hipster-bestowed crownings of jazz, which gave us William "Count" Basie and "Duke" Ellington, "Lady" Day and "Pres"

Lester Young. A celebration of in-crowd homage married to a public recognition of idiosyncrasy, such colourful nomenclature has always been a feature of African-American musical culture. (Today it continues to thrive in the MCs, Queens, Kings, Princes and Grandmasters of rap.) Throughout his career, James Brown would be aided by colleagues with expressive handles: men like Alfred "Pee Wee" Ellis, "Sweet" Charles Sherrell, John "Jabo" Starks, "Bootsy" Collins and his brother Phelps "Catfish" Collins, Richard "Kush" Griffith, Jimmy "Chank" Nolen, Frank "Kash" Waddy, "Half-Pint" Jackson, Hal "Cornbread" Singer, Alphonso "Country" Kellum, Hearlon "Sharp Cheese" Martin – and women like Vicki "Songbird" Anderson or singer/comedienne Elsie "TV Mama" Mae.

Such names were essential identities in an America which had long been "negro" but which would emerge, alongside Brown's stardom, newly born as *black*. These were titles, beings, selves which existed beyond the reach of another America: the world of birth and arrest records, tax documents, property deeds, draft registration and similar agencies of the (white) Man. Their history and culture – like their character, which juxtaposed the folksy with the grandiloquent, the diminutive with the magnificent – was proudly and defiantly oral. No one could nail it down or define it too narrowly . . . these names and their world, however public they happen to become, remain very much a matter of private black control.

Since the days of chattel slavery, name-shifting has been central to African-American consciousness. It partakes of two strands within black cultural expression: an ongoing tension between tradition and improvisation and a constant delight in oral performance – folk tales and storytelling through "signifying", "toasting" and "playing the dozens". (Variously known as "joining", "woofing" or "sounding", the *dozens* are rhymed, ritual insults exchanged among young, lower-class black males. *Toasts* are longer, narrative rhymes which feature folk or street characters and rude language; they are thought to have originated among prisoners and hoboes. *Signifying* is tactical talking – either as part of a verbal contest, or as a means of conveying one's information indirectly, by speaking "around" a subject.)

"For people denied social and economic power," writes John Michael Vlach in *The Encyclopaedia of Southern Culture*'s entry on "African Influences", "verbal power provides important compensation." In James Brown's youth, this truth resonated throughout the segregated communities of the South via preaching, salesmanship and gamesmanship, arguing, bragging, gossiping, speechifying and what later students of Black English would term "Fancy Talking". Today, the same power fuels the many permutations of rap – an art form whose youthful, inventive practitioners vindicate James Brown's personal pride in Black English as an eloquent and important language.

In a 1972 essay titled "Signifying, Loud-Talking and Marking", anthropologist Claudia Mitchell-Kernan touched on the link between black America's expertise in verbal expressive practice and James Brown's affinity for flamboyant names and slogans, when she noted that:

> ... the black concept of signifying incorporates essentially a folk notion that dictionary entries for words are not always sufficient for interpreting meanings or messages, or that meaning goes beyond such interpretations. Complimentary remarks may be delivered in a left-handed fashion. A

particular utterance may be an insult in one context and not in another. What pretends to be informative may intend to be persuasive. The hearer is thus constrained to attend to all . . . the total universe of discourse.

Language – literal *words* – would never be sufficient for all those things James Brown needed to convey. True communication, real involvement with fellow humans, resides in movement, tone, nuance and allusion as much as in what one says or sings. ("Now you *really sayin' somethin'*.") Equally, however, Afro-America knows that language itself is impoverished when it is robbed of richness and style – what linguist J L Dillard calls "the elements of conscious elegantizing: use of intentionally glittering and sesquepedalian words and phrases, and the type of disregard for dictionary precision of meaning which can be documented from many Afro-American sources."

Of all black America's expansive linguistic practices, many of the most exuberant reside in the powerfully syncretic Southern church, with its fusion of West African religious ritual and Anglo-European tradition. That church surrounded the young James Brown: in the form of fraternal "morality" or "harmony" organizations, "Refuge" churches, "Holiness Well Houses of Prayer", and "Universal Friendship Missions". Fiery, fantastical titles for bodies of worship abounded in his Southern childhood, just as they continue to do today – churches with names such as "Ark of Faith", "Love Sanctuary", "Strike Force International Assembly of God", "Learning As The Bible Speaks Assembly", "Church On Fire". In his 1976 monograph *Black Names*, J L Dillard observes how black churches differ from their white counterparts in that their names commemorate spiritual *aspirations*, rather than geographic locations. And today, when Brown speaks of the showmanship he absorbed from preachers like "Daddy" Grace or "Reverend Joe" May, he also mentions such houses of worship and their striking titles – like Bethlehem Fire Baptize Holiness Church of God of the Americas (nicknamed, says Dillard, "Daddy Grace's Church" or, according to James, "Bishop Grace's House of Prayer").

Brown took that African-American verbal delight in claiming, in personalizing, and made it an integral part of his showmanship. He brought this fullness in his black identity right to the fore – along with proudly processed hair, downhome church moans ("zoomin' ") and intricate choreography. His records are crammed with by-name jokes, ad-libs and exhortations . . . touches he knew would further involve every conceivable sector of the black American public.

"It was just the completely silly stuff we used to say," remembers Fred Wesley. "He'd yell out, 'Hey Fred, where are you from?' and I'd say, 'L.A.' 'L.A.?' 'Yeah – Lower Alabama'. And this got on the *record*! He put it out and it made me famous. Twenty years later, people come up to me all over the world and say – 'Hey, man! You're from *Lower Alabama*.' "

Style, Brown quickly discovered, held the key to consistent success. He could become the it man, the hit man, the new man, the superman – faster and badder and sharper than anyone else. Everywhere black America wanted to go – into the big cities, the glamorous theatres, the golden L-Dog Road Hogs (Cadillacs), even the white man's bedroom – Brown set out to get there first. And, to this end, his art became more ecumenical than that of any black artist before or since.

He stole Little Richard's pompadour and whipped it on to

greater things, an imperious crest of bravado. He took the pirouettes and the 1840s jig dancing of black minstrel star William Henry "Master Juba" Lane (so well-known, Charles Dickens extolled them), the 1913 Texas Tommy and the 1920s jazz vernacular of the Lindy Hop – and brought them back to create the JAMES BROWN, which, twenty years later, would make breakdancing possible. He mused upon the iconography of the segregated film circuit, the expressionist epics of his youth like 1947's *Ebony Parade* and Dizzy Gillespie's *Jivin' In BeBop* with its gymnastic, surreal dance routines, or Louis Jordan's 1948 *Reet Petite and Gone.* And he absorbed the way such artefacts moved from drama and repartee to music and dance, then back again.

Critic Donald Bogle has pointed out that these movies, which mesmerized Brown as a schoolchild, present a portrait of the Negro performer "who is also a person with offstage life, with cultural connections and roots he can always return to". Such "race films" (like R'n'B, produced by black stars for an all-black audience) succeeded best as "fundamental celebrations of black style". James Brown says that he saw in them – particularly in jump blues singer-saxophonist Jordan – "a way for me to get into the community".

It may seem remarkable to think that this icon of black America ever felt *outside* that community. But Brown grew up the poorest of children, hustling and scrambling, both for a living and for attention. Even the most basic institutions rejected the raggedy kid who lived in a house of ill-repute. At grade school, he was sent home for "insufficient clothes". His father's failure to come up with bribe money in Augusta, he says, condemned him to pass his teenage prime in prison. And his major memory of serving that time is still that, "come every Sunday, *I* was the one that no one came to see".

For such a youth, the only arm of the black community always open was the church. The upbeat, urbane world of slick, black, '50s showbiz would have been daunting to any short, dark, country boy. Especially one employed – like the post-prison Brown was by 1953 – as a smalltown janitor with a wife and son to support.

For ten full years after his '52 release, the spectre of parole constantly hovered above Brown's head – controlling where and how he could tour, and further undercutting his dreams. "For a *long*, long time," says Bobby Byrd, "James had to be back in Toccoa every Sunday for church and Monday morning to make parole."

Nevertheless, Brown pressed on, peddling "Please Please Please" with the Flames and cutting disc after disc. All were audibly pastiche versions of other hitmakers' strengths – from Hank Ballard's balladeering through Louis Jordan's comic rock-abilly, the Five Royales' smooth songs and Little Richard's ineffable brand of pizzazz (explicitly copied by James on 1957's "Chonnie-on-Chon").

A management breakthrough had come his way as early as '54. Little Richard, then a rising Georgia star but still washing dishes at the Greyhound bus depot, had passed Brown on to Clint Brantly, his regional manager. It was Brantly, Brown claims today, who added the soubriquet "Famous" to his backing band the Flames. The manager also convinced them to move from dusty, smalltime Toccoa to the more musically active Macon, where his operation was based. For church Sundays and parole Mondays – not to mention life as a family with Mrs Brown (the former Velma

Warren of Toccoa) and first son Teddy – Brown's relocation produced complications. Plus, it would take him two years of unremitting roadwork to reach the charts again: this time with the pleading gospel adaptation "Try Me".

As with "Please Please Please", legend holds that Federal Records president Syd Nathan hated "Try Me" – Brown had to cut acetate demos himself and pay their way onto radio before his own label would put it out. But, when the tune hit No1 on the R'n'B charts – as well as inching into the pop Top 50 – Brown was at last given concrete confidence. And one of his first endeavours was to tackle problems with Federal's lessor, King Records.

Critic Robert Palmer: "By 1964 . . . King was . . . failing to distribute and promote Brown's records on a scale commensurate with his popularity as a live performer. Brown retaliated by forming Fair Deal Productions, and by giving his next set of recordings to Smash, a subsidiary of Mercury. One of the sides included in the package was "Out of Sight", and with Mercury's more thorough and up-to-date distribution network behind it, the record became one of Brown's biggest hits, selling to white listeners as well as the blacks who had been supporting him for years." (*The Rolling Stone History of Rock and Roll*).

The legal result was a face-off which lasted one year. But, in the end, that battle rewarded Brown with almost unheard-of artistic command over what he would record and how it would then be marketed. In these business strategies, he was aided by a white man he came to describe as "the father I never had": the late Ben Bart, then a booking agent at New York's Universal Attractions.

The recommendation of Brown to Bart, whom Brown called "Pop" and who called him "Jim" or "Jimmy", had come through his renown as a live performer. Bart was a hands-on type who had managed, promoted, and booked national acts, even started an independent label of his own (Hub Records). He told James Brown – over and over – that Brown had something really special. But, Bart also warned the singer, it would never hit right off across the lines of segregation. "He knew it would take me time to reach the white listener," says James. "He told me that years ago. He said 'Jim, if you gonna live with 'em, you gotta teach 'em'."

By the end of the '50s, Brown was on the road to that bigtime of which he had dreamt. And, right through to the Apollo live album in 1962 (another project opposed by almost everyone to whom it was suggested), he was constantly redefining what live performance could mean. "*Live At The Apollo*" sold a million copies. And it made Brown's following single, the ballad "Prisoner of Love", into his first pop Top 20 hit. By the time he and Fair Deal Productions emerged from his battle for power with King, Brown had accrued a stack of R'n'B dance hits that included both the evocative "Night Train" and wild cry-singer ballads like "Lost Someone", "I Don't Mind", "Baby You're Right" and "Bewildered". He was also building a bi-racial public that, with "Out of Sight" in '64, would become international. And, just as his idol Louis Jordan had access to the savvy advice of Decca's white producer Milt Gabler, Brown could call on "Pop" Bart to co-design his celebrity.

The backwoods country boy had certainly come a long way. And rubbing shoulders with venerable acts from Hank Ballard to Ray Charles along segregation's so-called "chitlin circuit" wised Brown up to more than just performer/audience tricks. He also picked up fast on the hustling side – nurturing one-on-one relationships with DJs, local promoters and the proprietors of those Mom-and-Pop stores and barbershops where R'n'B tickets were sold and concerts publicized. For Brown, pre-eminence in this black media market – control over his life – held attractions more potent than the most forbidden drug.

The inimitable saxophonist Maceo Parker, who joined Brown's band in 1964, was fascinated by the breadth of the entertainer's control – as well as his instinctual savvy. "Not only did James Brown have the knack or the ability to sit down – if he took the time to sit down! – and schedule and program and publicize each show. He also had an almost uncanny, innate ability to judge character. Not just in musicians, either; in every kind of personnel. When James was building JAMES BROWN almost everyone offered potential to him. He didn't forget nobody where they might've helped."

Brown's drive, ex-colleagues agree, is something which passes description; it verges on the pathological. Maceo Parker: "His life became so amazin' – he went all the way to the top, and beyond. But he could never accept arriving. He always had one more place to go." And, by the end of the 1960s, Brown was uncorking things that showbiz had never quite seen before.

Fred Wesley, who joined in 1968: "Music was changing and *he* was changing it. James Brown changed everybody's ideas about music. Everybody." He cracks a smile. "It's like saying 'shit' and 'damn' on TV. Once somebody says it and the censor lets it slide, okay, it's gonna be everybody. Redd Foxx gets away with it, so there's Richard Pryor – and then you get Eddie Murphy.

"Once you get away with something, you've set a precedent. And back there in the '60s, James set a *hell* of a precedent. All music that we hear today is influenced by James Brown. I stand on that – everybody today who calls himself a creator of music has been influenced by James."

But Wesley alludes to theory and vinyl – and Brown's true test, his real pulpit, has always been the public stage. Consider early rock writer Nik Cohn's transliteration of James seen live as the full extent of his power began to dawn, both on him and on the public:

> His stage act lasts one full hour and all that time he's doing nothing but working up panic, hammering and hitting, shucking, falling to his knees like some cryman Negro Johnny Ray, striding the stage on bandy legs like some dwarfish Groucho Marx. And his band grinds on behind him and his dancers pirouette and his drummers lay about him. Then he goes into some dancing . . . tight black pants and legs like propeller shafts and he's only beautiful.
>
> On "Prisoner of Love" he walks away from the mike and calls the title in the darkness. Very thin and distant, repeating just these three words over and over. Then he comes back into the light, up to the mike, and he lets out a series of screams, mad anguished shrieks that last ten seconds each. Probably they're the loudest sounds you've ever heard any human being make and, physically, you can't not be moved by them. That's the way he works on you. That's the way he hurts and beats you up.
>
> Under all its gimmickry, *Cohn also wrote*, It's sexual and menacing and genuinely meant. It's also a black show, an Apollo show, and no white man could ever fully join in with it. (*Rock From The Beginning*).

James the Soul Surrealist had been born. And, just as Fred Wesley claims, music would not be the same again.

the surrealist who
came in from the snow

"What separates us from the blacks today is not so much the colour of our skin or the type of our hair as the phantom-ridden psyche we never see except when a black lets fall some cryptic phrase. It not only seems cryptic: it is so. The blacks are obsessionally complicated about themselves. They've turned their suffering into a resource."

Jean Genet, *The Prisoner of Love*, 1986

By 1965, Brown was really using the artistic control he had wrested from King through his long contractual wrangle. That summer, he scored his first Top Ten hit on the pop charts, with a revolutionary record entitled "Papa's Got A Brand New Bag". It was the sort of record – instant and self-announcing – for which Little Richard was famous. But, unlike Richard's one-off H-bombs, Brown's hit sounded like the initiation of a *programme*. And, for all the minimalism of its punchy rhythms, it purveyed a weird, intriguing seductiveness which lingered ("Come on – hey, hey!") long after the vocal faded. Brown was declaring what critic Dave Marsh has called "a new order of rhythm". He was also making it clear that the enterprise would rest on him: *Papa*, the linchpin and font – the Daddy-O of a fresh, dancin' generation.

Papa's follow up – "I Got You (I Feel Good)" – was destined to go even further, piercing the mainstream US lineup at No 3. And Brown was able to consolidate this crossover with appearances on TV – since 1955, a common appliance in most middle-income American homes. In the privacy of suburbia, the freestyle straightforwardness of his act might have blown the minds of whites who beheld it. But a new era was dawning in consumer-conscious America.

The twist dance craze had been initiated by Chubby Checker on Dick Clark's *American Bandstand* in 1960 (Chubby aka Ernest Evans was filling in for the song's creator, Brown's Federal label-mate Hank Ballard). And, in tandem with Tamla-Motown's onslaught of crossover singles, the Twist and subsequent phenomena – like Little Eva's '62 Locomotion; the Monkey, popularized by Major Lance in '63; or the Jerk, plugged during '64 by the Larks, the Contours, the Miracles and the Capitols, not to mention the Swim or the Barracuda – had tied America's *idea* of pop to inventive and novel dances. And the Twist, *American Bandstand* svengali Dick Clark observed, "had tremendous social significance. Overnight it became OK to be older and say you liked rock and roll."

Brown was R'n'B, not "rock and roll". But he knew the potential of dance as a crossover tool – and not just because of his gymnastic ability to leave an audience breathless. Late in '59, when King supremo Syd Nathan had refused to let him record an instrumental version of his Mashed Potatoes routine, Brown went behind his employer's back to Henry Stone's Miami-based Dade Records. There, using the name of his then drummer Nat Kendrick, he cut "Do The Mashed Potatoes, Parts 1 & 2" with disc jockey King Coleman's voice dubbed over his own. Credited to "Nat Kendrick and the Swans", the record made the US R'n'B Top Ten – and contributed its bit to the country's emerging dance-mania.

America's locomotive fad generated a host of national and local televised pop-and-dance shows during the '60s. And they proved perfect vehicles for Brown's bad bad whirligig self. The *TAMI Show* had made him a sought-after showman for the likes of *Bandstand, Where The Action Is*, and *The Lloyd Thaxton Show*, as well as more regional variants whose footage has not survived. Also, in 1965, Brown executed a special big-screen cameo: along with the Famous Flames, he appeared in a Frankie Avalon film vehicle titled *Ski Party*.

The picture was produced by American International – a company founded in '54 to specialize in teen-appeal packages which would portray US youth as decent rather than delinquent. But, by the time it reached *Ski Party*, AIP's "company policy" had degenerated to tease-and-sleaze product – and their formula was wobbling on its last legs. The movie which gave James Brown his widescreen break is therefore a crazy mixture. It transfers the beach-party narratives which preceded it to the ski-slopes, then spices that action with a *Some Like It Hot* subplot concerning two buddies in drag. (These parts were played by crooner Frankie Avalon and TV's *Dobie Gillis*, Dwayne Hickman.)

Brown's brief appearance is a hit-and-run affair, a Cubistic non-sequitur. Followed by the Flames and three Saint Bernard dogs (wearing kegs marked "Whiskey", "Vodka" and "Whatever You Got"), he invades an *après-ski* frug party through some patio windows. One of the many surrounding nubiles bounces up to him and brief, cardboard repartee is exchanged. The intruders' identities are speedily acknowledged ("I know who you really are! You're James Brown and the Flames! I have all your records!"). Then Brown gets down to business, performing "I Got You (I Feel Good)".

And the screen leaps into three dimensions, the silly set and dialogue fading away as James's fancy footwork threatens to set the fake flagstones alight. As he coils and uncoils his gestures with a consummate authority, Brown's shimmying ankles sweep him back and forth. He dips and clips the air, clearing three flights of stairs with two pirouettes and then descending to do it again. His forehead is a mountain of upswept bouffant curls which rival the Dynel accessories of the watching teen queens. His ski sweater (bottom button undone) is emblazoned with sequins. And his clumsy ski apparel reveals stretch pants and Cuban heels.

Among his chalet "audience", there are shots of calculated admiration and disbelief. But the real reaction took place across suburban America. As Brown, on one vibrating limb, exited backwards through the French windows then, with a forward kick and a split-second split in the "snow", disappeared, millions of white teens came face-to-face with Southern black cool, surrealist-style.

This was not the Harlem Apollo's James Brown ("I felt like I was in a straitjacket," the singer later observed.) But what *he* could do to a lyric like "I feel nice/like sugar and spice" was audibly different to what white popsters like Avalon or Lesley Gore (*Ski Party*'s other pop guest star) could accomplish. For the middle-American teens who would put "Out of Sight" and "Papa's Got a Brand New Bag" into the pop charts, there was clearly a mystery here. What lifted a man and slid him about as smoothly as if he wore roller skates? What gifted him with such effortless, totally throwaway charm? In the strange, secretly cynical world of teen-movie showbiz, Brown's regal bearing and grave sense of getting down looked like The Cool personified.

As for his touch of weirdness, the teen audience already had some experience of expressionistic extremes – thanks to a string of "morbid death" hits which enlivened their Top 40 playlist. The late '50s and '60s was a heyday for teen grief classics: songs which packed all the angst of adolescence into one metaphor – the Big Breakup of death. In overwrought numbers such as Mark Dinning's "Teen Angel" (a 1960 No 1), Jody Reynolds' "Endless Sleep" or Ray Peterson's "Tell Laura I Love Her" (a Top Ten entry in summer 1960), young lovers found themselves suddenly parted – beyond kissing and making up, beyond the comfort of a telephone call. Death was brutal and unpredictable – it could come via a stock car race, a plunge in the river, a race to retrieve one's class ring from the railroad track. Jan and Dean, whose '63–'64 heyday included the creepy "Dead Man's Curve" with its after-the-accident monologue reliving a gory car crash, would even appear on the *TAMI Show* with James Brown. Under the shadow of the Bomb, in the chill of the Cold War, apprehension, as well as exuberant dancing, had helped to define mainstream pop sensibility. Young white America wasn't totally unprepared for James.

Add to this that black celebrity was about to be redefined in the USA and one can see how Brown's persona was enhanced by historic events. No sooner had the singer broken through on American TV and radio, than he was perceived as part of an emerging cadre of strong, black men . . . men somehow sent to heal faults in the basic American conscience. During December of '64, Dr Martin Luther King had been awarded the Nobel Peace Prize. And soon many other names – Adam Clayton Powell, H Rap Brown, Andrew Young, Julian Bond, Black Panthers Huey Newton and Bobby Seale, a prisoner named George Jackson and a dynamic young reverend who shared his last name – would start to make first an impact, and then demands, on white America.

Whether he wished it or not, Brown was inescapably caught in the public's fears and preconceptions about these new celebrities. And gone forever was his initial dream of dignified, Louis Jordan-style crossover. Now America's black population was starting to make *real* noise. And, despite Brown's secret desire to become a "sepia Sinatra" (a persistent attraction which would reassert itself over and over in syrupy ballads and LPs like '69's *Getting Down To It*, or 1970's jazzy *Soul On Top*), he could see how the action was shaping up. His no-compromise showmanship, not to mention his huge black following, was soon used to make him – no question – America's Soul Brother No 1.

The Civil Rights movement caused the US to redefine its

perceptions of "the Negro". And, in parallel, James Brown was changing not just the *moment* of rhythm and blues and "soul", but the very conventions which constructed those musics. In the middle '60s, he moved from interpreting formal, traditional song styles to building a sound of his own. The "big band" he recruited to implement this vision – the James Brown Revue – had its roots in the hard-hitting Southwestern dance groups of Texas, Kansas City, St Louis and Oklahoma. From them he took the idea of a dense, blues-based machine, with a churning rhythm engine and brash brass punctuation. These were the kind of backing ensembles a singer *really* had to shout to front. But Brown's attraction to the screaming Southwestern saxophone and the honking "Texas Tenor" traditions was only part of his fascination for "jazz". To him, that word meant many things – from the traces of call-and-response he heard in Count Basie's band to the angular polyrhythms of be-bop, or the "jump" of Jordan's Tympany Five.

"My first influence was gospel," says Brown, "but my second influence is jazz. I do like some blues, but I don't really go too deep there. I prob'ly only really like two or three blues artists. I have pretty big jazz feelin's, though. I been right through that book.

"But I never try and express what I actually did," he adds. "I wouldn't try to do that, cause definition's such a funny thing. What's put together to make my music – it's something which has real power. It can stir people up and involve 'em. But it's just something I came to hear."

Pretty soon others were hearing this fresh and simple but radical sound – the music history would come to call funk. Like the word from which it stole the name (meaning a stench stemming from sex), *funk* betokened a turn-around about what was "polite" in black society. The impulse which could turn an impolite adjective into the ultimate term of approbation presaged a re-evaluation of roots – one which led to the '60s slogan "Black is beautiful". Further down the line, that same transformation would inspire the battle against a "Eurocentric" concept of culture.

"I do remember," laughs Maceo Parker, "havin' to get that term 'funk' OK'd by my parents, and some of my peers havin' to get it OK'd by *their* parents. I thought it was strange at the time, because parents just didn't really understand – they didn't know things to do with music. It was a generation gap. But, to them, it was just not a gentleman's word.

"See, when I got out of college," he adds, "it was just a way to play: funky as opposed to straight. Just a form, a style of music. *James* made it a craze."

Brown's change hinged on a style of drumming: a "funky" beat which came from New Orleans and was best exemplified in his Revue by a player named Clyde Stubblefield. Alfred "Pee Wee" Ellis, who joined Brown in '65, says it was already known to musicians as something called "New Orleans beat": "If, in a studio, you said 'play it funky' that could imply almost anything. But 'give me a New Orleans beat' – you got exactly what you wanted. And Clyde Stubblefield was just the epitome of this funky drumming. There was a way his beat was broken up; a combination of where the bass and the snare drums hit which was topsy-turvy from what had been goin' on.

"But *James*," adds Ellis, "did a tune early in the '60s called 'I Got Money'. And *it's* funky. For him, the thing was always there."

Under bandleader Nathaniel "Nat" Jones, hired in 1964, Brown had begun to project a tough, conceptual sound – songs which were downhome and immediate, but, at the same time, poetically resonant. But this project received its de facto public premiere in 1965, with "Papa's Got A Brand New Bag". "I really can't remember what was in my mind, where I got all that stuff," Brown confesses on film years later in *The James Brown Story*. "But I knew I had something. And when they played it, that was *it*: it just destroyed all the other arrangements."

What is this thing called funk? Well, in "Papa", while alternating choogling, choked-out bursts of guitar with sharp stabs of brass, Brown exhorts listeners as if he were punching them. He lumps dance crazes of the past (the Jerk, the Fly, the Boomerang, the Monkey, the Mashed Potatoes) in with corny slang ("see you later, alligator"), but he gives the central nod to "the new breed thing" he himself personifies.

Though less forceful and groundbreaking than "Papa" itself, the series of funky singles which followed were ingenious and constantly changing. The sharply-delineated "I Got You (I Feel Good)", issued four months after "Papa", underscores Brown's visceral, torn-paper voice by emphasizing the elegance of his timing. And the looser-limbed "Ain't That A Groove" of February '66 features Brown's advice to the lovelorn set in front of expansive, big-band backing and a supportive female chorus. That summer's "Money Won't Change You" serves up weird, choppy vocal incantations ("Money won't change you / money won't change you / money won't change you / but time will take you OUT"). All three are underwritten by a building, chugging groove – the funk – whose gravity feels as tenacious as the teeth of an angry pit bull.

By the late '60s, those tensions epitomized in the push-and-pull of Brown's "new bag" were all around him: in his band and in the country. "As the money got bigger," says Bobby Byrd, "let's put it this way – the attitudes changed. James didn't remember that we were all there for each other. He forgot who first went to bat for him, who got him out of prison, who took him into their home. He forgot who helped create his thing; he started to think it was *all* him."

Byrd pauses delicately, reaching back to the church for a metaphor which will help him out. "I think it's one of his failings – you get too big and you forget the bridge that bring you over."

"Everything really worked around James," explains later arrival Maceo Parker. "And you had to think quick to keep up. A lot of solos, for instance, were just impromptu. He calls out your name, you just had to throat it, then hope it's kinda relative to what is goin' on.

"It all worked around how *he* felt," he continues. "In the studio, for instance, he wanted to be hip to everything goin' on. So he was really into 'bring this up, bring this down' – all that stuff."

Parker is a man with a well-seasoned spark in his eye. "It got to a point," he says, "where you don't know if what he's thinkin' *now* is what he's thinkin' next week. This led to a lot of 'I didn't say that! I didn't hum that!' 'Yes, you did, Mr Brown.' 'No, I *didn't*!' – you know? When what's actually happening is -- he's forgot the part he said to play. But, look, he's still the boss. We all went through that a lot." Parker smiles. "That's why I bought me a tape recorder. Cause I couldn't write things down as fast as Pee Wee or Fred Wesley."

Zig-zagging round the country, stumbling from gigs to the studio, working and seething, then working and letting off steam with prodigious partying, the James Brown Revue caught the mood of its time. A mood which would, in '66, be characterized by two words: Black Power.

Savouring those words four years later, Kent State University historian August Meier pegged the movement as a culmination – the inevitable result of black impatience with every facet of American life: "Disillusionment with the national administration and with white liberals, the fragmentation of the Negro protest movement, the enormous difficulties which stood in the way of overcoming the problems of the black masses, and the riots that erupted spontaneously in 1964 and 1965 as a consequence of the anger and frustration of the urban slumdwellers – all set the stage for the dramatic appearance of the black power slogan in the summer of '66." (*Black Protest in the Sixties*).

James Brown was reaching his own, parallel culmination, learning where his strength really lay as opposed "to where people had told me I would find it". Instead of the solo singer's traditional backing band, he welded the restive Revue into a seamless extension of his ever-enlarging self – one able to trade riffs and rhythmic emphases with remarkable grace and speed. And, among the endless rehearsals, the fines, the ceaseless discipline and exhaustion with which he kept over thirty people on the road eleven months a year, there was still pride in the total achievement. "We were the onliest one that started out with that big band," says Bobby Byrd. "Sayin' 'we'll orchestrate it, we'll take it *big*' – lookin' good, like Louis Jordan. We were the very first in our era. Then Otis Redding, he got him one, then Joe Tex, then the others. But we were the first to say 'we're gonna see *our* stuff writ large'."

The creative ferment between James Brown and those sidemen

he recruited was keen. Alfred "Pee Wee" Ellis, his bandleader after '65, would become the first formal co-architect of the funk. A be-bop aficionado whose formative years were spent among the uninhibited honkers of the Texas Panhandle, Ellis was playing a Miami lounge act ("carnival bands, rock bands, R'n'B – the beach was a trip down there!") when he caught Brown's ear. Some months after, in Rochester, New York, Revue trumpeter Waymond Reed rang him up.

At leisure in a tracksuit and a jaunty fedora twenty years on, Pee Wee is sanguine as he strokes his chin and transports himself back in time. What led him to James *was* James, he says. The musical challenge and sheer, overwhelming showbiz Brown represented whet even the appetite of a youthful, snappily-dressed jazz snob.

"I'm a curious kind of guy," says Pee Wee – who served as Van Morrison's musical director for seven years after leaving Brown. "I'm lookin' for the odd angle every time. Waymond called me up and said, 'Listen, you know who James Brown is?' And I said, 'Yeah – kinda.' Cause he was some other stuff for me; I'd been studying Sonny Rollins."

But Waymond was offering $250 a week, and Ellis' self-confessed curiosity eventually got the better of him. "I went down to Washington DC and over to the Howard Theatre. And I stood backstage for about a week, watching the James Brown show. And – that shit really blew my mind! GOD DAMN! It was a fantastic show. I was only twenty-four and I was wild and crazy, too. So for me it was like, let's *go*. Six months later, I was the bandleader."

Pee Wee's gungho enthusiasm – a musically erudite comple-ment to Brown's own insatiable hunger for progress – spelled the end for then-supremo Nat Jones. "I couldn't keep my mouth shut," Ellis admits. "I was 'try this, try that' all the time. And the band would just light up." When Brown found Jones was handing his charts on to Pee Wee, he made the change official.

"We were playing every night, just *cranking* this shit out," says Ellis. "And I was totally excited all the time. I was there in the back of the tour bus with the lights on. Workin', workin', workin'. Cause I knew that when we stopped, we were really gonna get on it."

"Did we pick up speed?" Pee Wee looks incredulous. "Yeah, man, the speed of *light.* When you heard James Brown was comin' to town, you stopped what you were doin' and started saving your money. Cause you know that you're goin', ain't no debate about it. 'James Brown's comin' – OK, see you there.' We were *it*, you see. And EVERYBODY WENT."

Ellis is not just boasting. By the late '60s, Brown's Revue had become a heavy-duty locomotive of groove, striking sparks off every track it touched as it crossed – and conquered – the States. And Brown himself was in constant motion: recruiting, rehearsing, refining, *reacting.* He was building a whole, stylized world – and the injection of Ellis's jazz-schooled feeling for polyrhythm gave him the chance to place his adventurous instincts right at the heart of the enterprise. The first song Ellis says he wrote with Brown was "Let Yourself Go" – "which is where 'There Was A Time' came from". And therein lay a major change which came to fruition during summer '67, with the duo's most famous collaboration: the tune entitled "Cold Sweat".

"Let Yourself Go" is a funk primer whose vocal proclaims its history: "Let me tell you the news . . . It ain't just soul, it's Rhythm 'n' Blues." And "Cold Sweat" realized its potential – fusing an extended jam of like Southern minds into a turbine groove, a groove which seems at once to move forward and to churn in place. Embellished with choppy, frenetic scrabblings of guitar, here – two years after "Papa" – was definitive funk. Like all the best African-American music, it is utterly immediate. But, more than that, its musical fabric is at one with that all-out Southern surrealism Brown's lyrics capture: "In my home town where I used to stay / The name of the place – HA! – is Augusta, GA / Down there / we have a good time / we don't talk – HA! / We all get together, in any type of weather, then do / the camel walk." ("There Was A Time", December 1967).

Funk is not a reconciliation of opposite rhythmic impulses, but the fusion and transcending of their essential *conflict.* And that Brown/Ellis breakthrough was saluted by the public when "Cold Sweat, Parts 1 & 2" became an R'n'B No 1 – as well as a No 7 hit on the pop charts. The triumph was further consolidated in May '68, when their "Licking Stick – Licking Stick, Parts 1 & 2" rose to No 2 on the R'n'B chart and No 14 in the pops.

Again, "Licking Stick" highlighted Brown's surreal modus operandi: the way he could assimilate everyday language to spell out, then sell, a vision – *his* vision – of the world. Critics often focus on Brown's percussive phrasing and use of the lyrics, the way his words are hammered or dropped or flung away, in deference to the ruling rhythms. But equally striking and very much his own, *après* funk, is the way Brown's music reverberates with a sense of the basic power in language.

To him, repetition, slogans, sentence constructions and semi-random strings of words are raw material every bit as potent as the beats behind and beneath them. Sometimes Brown's wordplay functions like the rhapsodic invocation of a religious spell. At others, it presents as revelation the phenomena mainstream culture would relegate to the margins – what critic Francesco Pellizzi terms "totally suppressed identities". In the case of James Brown, of course, such suppressed identities form the very heartbeat of his black America. But in lyrics as hyper-real as these from "Licking Stick", Brown endows them with a striking, completely spontaneous character: "People standing / Standin' in a trance / Sister out in the backyard / doin' her outside dance / Come tellin' me the other day / She didn't wanna be a drag / I don't know what she's doin' / Think she's got a brand-new bag."

Put together by Brown, Ellis and Brown's old friend Bobby Byrd, "Licking Stick" is a single-chord funk mantra which, underscored by skeletal horn lines, manages to sound both minimal and hallucinatory. Yet its musical structure is only part of the story. Much of the tune's impact is due to the utter completeness with which Brown gave himself to performing – not just this track, but everything he sang. His was a totally rapt transmogrification: the thing teenage Gerri Hirshey and pre-pubescent Michael Jackson interpreted as possession. And it was part of what Brown's employees had to translate into "sound". James did not chart or arrange his own compositions – and there were serious limits to the technical specifics he was able to convey. It was up to his various bandleaders to deliver, onstage or in the studio, what Brown "heard" in his head.

"I had to learn enough about James Brown's style, direction and concept," says Pee Wee Ellis today, "to make that translation for him. Which is sort of an archaeological thing. You want to preserve the basic findings. But you also want to see what it is, to understand and analyze it – so it will last forever. So you can build on it and expand.

" 'Let Yourself Go' for instance," he says. "If you listen to that you can analyze it. See where really slight musical introductions of jazz and classical theory and stuff start creeping in. Same sound, now – but different chords. That piece of music is a monument to where things started to change. It allowed James Brown to go on to another level of class." Pee Wee pauses. "And he *went on*, too."

Indeed he did. Between '66 and '68, as he became a kind of folk politician, Brown's world exploded. He leased a private jet (and had "Out of Sight" emblazoned along its fuselage). He endorsed the mainstream NAACP – The National Association for the Advancement of Colored People – onstage at the Harlem Apollo. He flew to the hospital bedside of James Meredith when that Civil Rights integrationist was shot on his March For Freedom in Mississippi. He played shows which benefitted SNCC – Stokely Carmichael's radical Student Non-Violent Co-Ordinating Committee – as well as Dr King's more moderate Southern Christian Leadership Convention. He also met and campaigned for Vice-President Hubert Humphrey – a bizarre yet enduring relationship sparked, according to Brown, by his 1966 recording of "Don't Be A Dropout". (Today, in his wallet, Brown still carries a tattered xerox "testimonial" from the late HH.)

Brown publicly endorsed the sort of black capitalism he practised. But *his* form of Black Power, he says, was togetherness and self-improvement. "I was never into black power," he told journalist Christina Patoski in 1982. "I was black pride. It's different, power and pride. That's why I always pushed the word pride. What influence I had over people is not power. Power's what ruin people. *God* has power; human bein' has influence."

Yet, in the eyes of even the Black Panthers (who were leaning on him to become more militant), Brown was the incarnation of the African-American soul. He was a one-man demonstration of how deep the codes and meaning of music run in black America, how they evoke an historic continuum, how they can move to unite. During December of '68, Adrian Dove alluded to this, as he attempted an explication of "soul" for the *New York Times.*

"For the brother," wrote Dove, "music is important. He can be moved by soul music for days. At a theatre where, say, Soul Brother Number One, rhythm and blues singer James Brown is into his act, performer and audience are not separate from one another. They're together, they feel as one, and the music is made up to fit the mood right there and then. You know this moment will never happen again. But you don't have to be at a theatre to feel it . . . Wherever I go, if my day has been foul, I can turn on my transistor radio and everything is mellow."

Brown's heavy reputation was both underwritten and enhanced by the virtuosity of the Revue's major musicians – men like Ellis, sax players Maceo Parker, St Clair Pinckney and L D Williams, trumpet players Waymond Reed and Joe Dupais, guitarists Jimmy Nolen and Alphonso Kellum – and "funky drummers" Clyde Stubblefield and John "Jabo" Starks. It was a cast which would swell and shrink with the vicissitudes of its employer's unpre-dictable ego, causing his British friend and hagiographer Cliff White to note, circa '77, that "at the last count nearly 70 musicians have flowed through the corporate identity, making the personnel turnover of vocal groups like the Platters or the Drifters seem slow by comparison . . . This hive of talented discontentment has fostered quite an impressive alumni of ex-JB musicians: like the MD/arranger/writers; JC Davis (saxes) the leader of Brown's first band who went on to work with Etta James; Al "Brisco" Clark (saxes) who went on to work with Otis Redding; Nat Jones (saxes, keyboards) who went into a mental home; Alfred "Pee Wee" Ellis (saxes, keyboards, guitar, bass) who went on to become a respected session musician/arranger; Richard "Kush" Griffith (trumpet) who went on to obscurity and, of course, Maceo Parker (saxes, keyboards, flute) and Fred Wesley (trombone, keyboards) who are both currently flirting with George Clinton's Parliafunkadelicment thang."

There were and would be many other famous Brown "alumni": William "Bootsy" Collins and his brother Phelps; drummer Frankie "Kash" Waddy, flugelhorn player Haji Akhba – not to mention the Revue roster of great female vocalists: Yvonne Fair, Tammi Terrell, Lyn Collins, Marva Whitney, Martha High, Vicki Anderson.

But, in 1968, the focus on Brown himself was approaching its zenith. And, on top of the ferment within black America, "Top 40" music was also changing. The sway of English R'n'B copyists – such as Brown fans the Beatles and the Rolling Stones, today referred to by James as "the boys, the *major groups*" – was yielding to heavier, denser sound, sound as pure "experience". Sly and the Family Stone were attempting a democratic, multi-racial, pop-styled version of Brown's Revue. And Jimi Hendrix was pushing his personal psychedelicized sonic *thang.* Like James Brown, Hendrix over-ran the 3-minute single format on which Top 40 pop charts (introduced in 1955 and based on *Billboard* magazine's "Hot Hundred") depended.

"We knew what we were doin' in the '60s and '70s was very different," says Maceo Parker whose tenure with Brown has lasted on and off for two decades. For many, Parker epitomizes the blend of skill and personality which has characterized Brown's best sidemen – now often known by the umbrella title "JBs".

Standing barefoot in a borrowed London kitchen thirty-three years after the fact, reheating chicken and rice for a 4 pm breakfast, Maceo claims it is *humour* which has carried him through the punishing schedules and ego injuries for so many years. "See, I always liked dancin' and movin' and actin' silly. And somehow I could corral all that into the music that James was doin'. This music was an art form; it could take everything in. And that was what appealed to me."

That, and the X factor of an extraordinary showmanship. Parker was still in high school when he first encountered James Brown – in Kinston, North Carolina. "This is a *very*, very small town! But it seemed like everyone I knew from a hundred-mile radius round it was there. And what I noticed was sheer EXCITEMENT."

Maceo pauses over his cooking. "I had viewed a lot of people already," he says, "and all of 'em had they own style: Jackie Wilson, Sam Cooke, Ray Charles, Little Richard. They were all doin' somethin' different – and all of it was exciting. But James, he already had just some little extra something. And it wasn't necessarily singin'. It had more to do with performing itself.

"I could sit and watch his show and *see* him take the level of excitement – and just keep it at a point. Keep it at a point and then bring it up a little bit, then bring it back *down*, then move it right back up. He had real control, real rapport with people's emotions – right there *as they changed* within the progress of one song! And by the time it was over, man, he really, really had 'em. I would look round – at church-goers and school-teachers – and everywhere was just FRENZY!"

Maceo's massive sideburns still shake with awe. The musician most closely identified with Brown (not least because of the music James has made by continuously invoking his name –

"Maceo! MACEO!" "Blow it Ma-CEO; brother, blow!" down the decades), Parker figured he saw his destiny when he saw Brown on that neighbourhood stage. "I'd been playin' since fifth grade, the age of eleven. But I was tryin' to get a handle on audience reaction, participation. I had to find out if I could deal with that.

"Cause James Brown's music is very simple. Sure it was nice and funky. But it's essentially simple stuff, not hard basic changes. I could tell there was something else; something much, much bigger. That's where *style* comes in – style and the application of theories."

Discuss Brown's watershed '60s and '70s music with almost anyone who helped devise it, and lots of abstract nouns crop up. Words like "vision", "concept", "theory", "style", "showmanship". But discuss the work with Brown himself and the father of funk, like most conceptual artists, becomes both concrete and direct. "Funk was not a project," he growls. "It happened as part of my ongoing thing. In 1965, I changed from the upbeat to the downbeat. Simple as that, really. I wasn't going for some known sound, I was aimin' for what I could *hear*. 'James Brown Anticipation' I'd call it. You see, the thing was *ahead*."

"Anticipation" is certainly apposite – Brown's music, once he found it, was a groove which could build and build, a groove which encircled and recapped its rhythms, so nothing was ever an end that wasn't also a new beginning. A groove as circular as its drums – a hypnotic means of celebrating the one-ness and present tense of African-American life. Or, as Brown says, "it's a *now*-ness." Just like the religion which informs his most elemental apprehension of life – and the sexuality which celebrates his all-too-mortal being – James Brown's groove is not an either/or but an all-in-all proposition. James Brown

Anticipation can take you higher and higher and higher; then start all over and take you there again. As with church itself, there was no *end*: this was meant to be music that would move the brother and sister "for days". It was part of your black life, it *was* black life. And, as with real religion, you are meant to carry it out of the temple and with you into the daily arena of temptation, jubilation and despair.

Would James Brown himself agree? "I think so. I was interested in humanity, in what would bring people together. What has always interested me is helping people learn to survive."

"People talk a lot about the repetition thing," says Brown. "But feelin' is never repetitious. I've said *that* again and again! That's a thing you learn in church: feelin' is spontaneous, feelin' is true, feelin' is soul. For me, feelin' has always provided the key to my survival."

During the 1960s and early '70s, Brown's touch seemed so certain it dazzled new recruits as much as his towering ego bruised them. How did he – a man who relied on "real" musicians completely to implement his ideas – pick and choose his accomplices with such unwavering success?

Pee Wee Ellis says he had "an inner ear". Ellis drums a be-ringed finger on the desk before him and savours the very words. "James has this instant ability, this basic mother-wit, which allowed him to apprehend a certain combination of things. And he could get close enough to accomplishing the spirit of it himself to figure 'if I can get this close, I can PUSH it the rest of the way'."

Fred Wesley, the legendary trombonist who succeeded Ellis as bandleader and spawned Brown classics like "Funky Drummer" (1970), "Doin' It To Death" (1973) and "Soul Power" (1971), puts it another way. He always found the right technical go-between, says Wesley – a musician who could transfer what James played, explained and described into organized charts and notes.

Wesley: "He knew what he needed and he would always find one person, a Pee Wee, to mediate between him and the band. *He* couldn't give it to the band directly, no way. You got a belly dancer, a horse and an apple? You give that directly to the band and one of 'em's going to try and make it with the belly dancer, someone else gonna ride the horse, and someone's gonna eat the apple. It won't come out *music*, right? You give it to someone like Pee Wee, let him run it through his brain, let him give it to them *as music*, and it'll come out a song.

"James knew he had to have that person," says Wesley. "But when he realizes he relies on you, he then resents you also. So we're right back to that insecure thing of his."

The question of Brown's personnel recruitment remains one of funk's most fascinating conundrums: how and where were those optimum players found at just the right time? Mostly, his staffing took place at second- or third-hand, through somebody already with the Revue. Sometimes, as with Ellis and Parker's brother Melvin, hired in '64 with Maceo as part of the package (Brown: "I didn't know what I had got!"), the draftees were people James had already heard. But, equally often, say Revue exes, musicians arrived as friends-of-friends. What surprised long-term onlookers like Maceo was the manner in which Brown exercised his final judgments. He had, says Parker, a truly mystical grasp on every angle by which his operation would be defined.

"A friend would usually pass on a friend," says Parker. "But if the chemistry wasn't there, James would just sit – or stop, standin'. And stare, and ask the guy some questions – really irrelevant stuff.

And, depending on what a guy was wearin', on what he had to say, on how he *walked* or whatever, James could make a decision – and be right."

Maceo frowns. "For years I tried to figure that out. For instance, just why did he use ME? I mean, everybody was playin', everybody was there. It could have been 'St Clair! St Clair!' But, all of a sudden, it's 'Maceo! Maceo!' I think of that a lot. Cause I tried to have a different thing goin', I tried to create my own style quote unquote. But," he shakes his head slowly, "I didn't think it was *that* different. Not to where it would suddenly be 'Oh yeah, gonna use THIS guy, gonna use him ALL the time'."

"The whole spectrum of James' concept," he says, "was to me quite amazing. Christ, how could he *know?*"

Confidence, say some JBs. Smarts, says Pee Wee Ellis; native smarts and "strong basic elements" driven by a relentlessly restless soul. "Cause James is indeed driven, he needs to be goin' somewhere all the time. Plus, he came up against serious competition in Jackie Wilson, Otis Redding, Wilson Pickett and them. For him to rise above these guys, he had to offer something else – and he had to get it out there FAST. Hence the whole production idea: uniforms, organization, strict rules. A bona fide CLASS ACT. The man had a vision and went for it. And he did not change his mind for *nobody*."

showdown in stylesville

"Who dat, knockin' at de do'? Why Ike Johnson, fu' sho'! Come in Ike, I'se mighty glad You come down. I t'ought you's mad at me 'Bout de othah night, An' was stayin' away fu' spite. Say now, was you mad fu' true W'en I kin' o' laughed at you. Speak up, Ike, and 'spress yourself."

Paul Laurence Dunbar

"... And there were Ferrari automobiles sitting in the ground 50 million years ago,
... and there were James Brown records sitting in the ground 50 million years ago,
... and there was acrylic paint flying through the air 50 million years ago. . ."

"Interviews", The Alpha Band, 1976 (Arista)

"Everybody's created equal," says James Brown, "but they don't *exercise* that thing."

In 1968, at the height of despair over political and racial divisions in America, Brown found himself besieged on all sides. His public standing had become so singular that everyone from LBJ to Rap Brown sought the potency of his backing: both as a conduit to his "people" and as a symbol in itself. Robert Farris Thompson, one of the world's chief authorities on African art and African-American aesthetics, recalls how, thirteen years later, he stumbled across a tape of Brown and Hubert Humphrey from that era: "I was in Brussels, coming back from Africa. It was 1981. I'm exhausted and I traipse into some motel on the outskirts of the big Brussels airport. Slink into my room, turn on the TV, and to my amazement there's a program on James Brown – in English with French and Flemish subtitles.

"Apparently, in '68, someone told Humphrey it might be a good thing if he was seen with James. And the footage of this was incredible. Because James was preaching to his people: 'Here is my man, you *NEED* to have him, he's my friend, he's a righteous man, he's THERE!' Then the camera swivels to Humphrey and up turns this bland countenance, with NO sense of resynchronizing his body language to this... *volcano* next to him. If ever there was a moment to tell you Humphrey was a loser, that was it! It was one of the most interesting juxtapositions I've ever seen: the style of James Brown in all-out confrontation with the straightest of white America."

On April 5, 1968, when Martin Luther King was assassinated, Brown no longer had time to ponder the weight of his role. Within twenty-four hours, in one of his life's signal moments, he turned a pre-scheduled Boston concert into a living plea for peace in the black community. Broadcast live by last-minute arrangement, his ploy was so successful in cooling city streets that the tape was run again the moment Brown's performance had ended. It was not the first or last time James's voice would be used to ice anger and violence – with slogans like *Don't Terrorize, Organize* and *Don't Burn, Learn*. And the following weekend, the singer flew to Washington DC, where disorder had been especially destructive – and there continued his pleas for restraint via live TV and radio.

Shortly after, Brown "met with" the US President (Lyndon Johnson). He then flew his band to Vietnam, leaving behind him a new record – a "patriotic rap" called "America Is My Home". This trio of events poured gasoline on the flaming rhetoric of black militants, who pictured the contradictory icon as an assimilationist, an Uncle Tom. After all, Brown's work had – to use a Hollywood term – made crazy bank during the '60s. And the conspicuous rewards he had accrued – the jet, the radio stations he owned, his mansion in St Albans, New York – hardly helped discredit complaints that James had bought into a system ruled by the Man. But even the censure of militants could not check Brown's record sales among blacks. On the contrary, his every new release was received by soul's core audience as half of an ongoing dialogue.

First used by literary figures such as author Richard Wright, the term "Black Power" had been brought to political prominence in Greenwood, Mississippi, during June, '66, by SNCC's Stokely Carmichael. But in its three syllables echoed the words of Malcolm X, spoken two years before: "Revolution is never based on begging somebody for an integrated cup of coffee. Revolutions are never based on love-your-enemy and pray-for-those-who-spitefully-use-you. Revolutions are never compromising. Revolutions overturn systems. And there is no system on this earth which has proven itself more corrupt, more criminal, than this system that in 1964 still colonizes 22 million African-Americans, still enslaves 22 million African-Americans."

A year after framing those sentiments, the former Malcolm Little was dead. And, during the next three years, as *US News & World Report* noted on November 13, 1967, 101 major riots had occurred in US cities, killing 130 people and injuring 3,673. The damage would total $714.8 million. And King's assassination quickly upped the ante: more cities were paralyzed, more people hurt, more homes and businesses and communities destroyed. Meanwhile, the body count from Vietnam was increasing.

When Brown entered the studio in Los Angeles during summer '68, all these things were on his mind. So was the expanding charisma of America's young, ultra-macho Black Power figureheads – celebrities who used black style to animate their romance of revolution. Brown cut "Say It Loud – I'm Black and I'm Proud" as *his* statement, his answer record to Stokely Carmichael and company: it was his demonstration that JAMES BROWN still spoke from the heart of black America, and for the street.

Characteristically, the song framed his demands for the race in personal, individual experience: "I worked on a job with my feet and my hands / But all the work I did / was for the other man / Now we demand a chance / to do things for ourselves / we're tired of beatin' our head against the wall / And workin' for someone else." The refrain of the title came in two parts: Brown's command to "Say it loud!" and the reply from a chorus of children (most, as he confessed in 1987, either Asian or white): "I'm black and I'm proud!" The song also included one line which, in later years, Brown would blame for the loss of many white listeners – "We'd rather die on our feet / Than live on our knees."

Later, Brown would come up with lyrics whose political analyses were more literal, like those of 1969's "I Don't Want Nobody to Give Me Nothing (Open Up the Door, I'll Get It Myself)" or 1974's speeded-up funk syncopation "Hell". Both contain inspirational verse lamenting the limits of opportunity in Black America. (*1969*: "I don't want nobody to give me nuthin' / Open up the door — HUH! / I'll get it myself, DO YOU HEAR ME? . . . Don't give me integration, give me true communication / Don't give me sorrow, I want equal op-por-tun-ity / To live tomorrow! / Give me schools – HA! – and better books / So I can read about myself and gain / my true looks." And, in *1974*: "It's HELL tryin' to make it when you're doin' it by yourself! / It's HELL payin' taxes when there's no money left / It's HELL givin' up the best years, the best years of your soul / Payin' dues / From the day you're born – GOOD GOD!") But "Say It Loud" articulated that status Brown had consolidated across Afro-America. And it made his stature as a black icon explicit to white listeners. Though the contemporary pop charts reverberated with Motown hits and with the soulsters of Atlantic and Memphis (Aretha Franklin, Solomon Burke, Wilson Pickett, Otis Redding and co), "Say It Loud" set James Brown apart once again. As a consequence, he would not see the inside of pop's Top Ten again for seventeen long years – until 1985 and *Rocky IV*'s "Living in America".

"Why was all that so important to me? Because I came from a very poor neighbourhood, a very poor element," he said in 1989. "And I had to suffer the *political* problems of my community. Those problems brought many people down; they still do it today. When I was growin' up, if somebody called me "black" that had an ignorance to it, a thing particular to itself. So when I was able to sing "Say It Loud, I'm Black And I'm Proud", it meant something special to ME. And it carried some weight."

At the same time, Brown made another sacrifice. It was one to which white America paid little attention, but one which stunned his own people. To convince movement moderns that he was a bona fide "natural man", James Brown sheared off his luxuriant, processed hair.

"I cut off my hair in Los Angeles, on Linden Boulevard," he told reporter Christina Patoski. "I remember that very well. Cause I showed 'em that this didn't hold me back. That it weren't the hair that make the mind. They said, 'How's he gonna be black if he don't cut his hair?' So, I *cut* my hair." On the 1982 National Public Radio recording, you can still hear Brown's laugh drowning halfway down his throat. "And I ain't gonna cut it again UNTIL I'M GOOD AND READY!"

James Brown's art has always been as much a politics of gesture as a matter of polyrhythm. And in those orbits, dress and toilette play a central, unambiguous role. "Hair and teeth," stated Brown firmly in his 1987 autobiography. "A man got those two things, he's got it all." The idea of high, high hair, curled and sculpted, first came to Brown via Little Richard and "Prince of the Blues" Billy Wright – a late '50s regular at prestigious black clubs such as Atlanta's Royal Peacock Lounge. In *his* 1984 autobiography, Little Richard recalls Wright wore "very loud clothin' and shoethin' to match his clothin' and wore his hair curled." Its stature was achieved through that straightening, neutralizing and curling procedure current in black life for twenty years – a system which conferred its name ("the process") onto the end result. (This was also termed, when James Brown was young, "made hair".) By the 1930s, such tall pompadour 'dos were known as "conks" – supposedly a hipster contraction of the popular straightening lotion whose name was *No More Kinks*.

Conks could be home-engineered (following directions like those in *The Autobiography of Malcolm X*, which feature lye, potatoes, high heat and a cream to safeguard the scalp). Or they could be coaxed up in that bastion of machismo, the black American barbershop. Either way, a lot of care was needed to straighten scientifically – lest the client be left with disaster and a frizzled scalp. Connoisseurs of the process were usually men who relished the social buzz of barbershops: places which bridged a gap between the velvet night of clubland and the dreary, 24–7 grind of daily domestic reality. "There is no place like a Negro barbershop," said black author and critic Ralph Ellison in a 1961 interview, "for hearing what Negroes really think. There is more unselfconscious affirmation to be found there on a Saturday than you can find in a Negro college in a month."

"The brother of the '50s," contends journalist Emory Holmes II, "transformed the conk into a uniquely black mode of expression, as different from the white styles that had inspired it as the music of Tin Pan Alley was different from bop." (*'King Konk', LA Weekly, 1988.*) And for '50s and '60s entertainers like Brown and Little Richard Penniman, black men on their way up from Southern juke joints to Harlem's Apollo, the lustrous, extravagant conk was a token of their determination.

It signified several things: that one had the leisure to build and maintain it, the glamour to carry it off and the money to keep it "right". The GI crewcut ("flat-top") and Cab Calloway marcel wave were styles blacks had to share with Caucasians. But the high-flying conk, with its requisite baptism of fire and flamboyant results, offered more deeply black credentials. Throughout the '50s and '60s, it ran a series of variations on who and what mattered inside Afro-America's socio-creative elite – rising from the scalps of boxers, bluesmen, "sepia spieler" DJs and jazz greats. But conks, just like James Brown himself, were really beyond the law. What they denoted was aesthetic certitude – plus a spirit of true improvisation.

Until he married third wife Alfie (née Adrienne Rodriguez), a hairdressing and makeup specialist he met on US TV's *Solid Gold*, Brown has been known to claim only one man ever got his hair "really right". This is Henry Stallings, a country boy from Georgia James has known since his own street-urchin days. Stallings made his way up north, where he briefly worked as Sugar Ray Robinson's sparring partner. When he gave up life as a punching bag, Stallings shifted to Robinson's Harlem barbershop. (Perhaps the same Harlem barbershop where Jean Genet heard Brown's "Prisoner of Love", providing him with a title for his meditation on terror and sex.) Reunited with Brown in New York, Stallings' triple-crown of connections – childhood, boxing and HAIR – made him the perfect minder for Mister Dynamite's 'do.

As James Brown's star has ascended, so have his hairdressing bills. By 1982, *Parade* magazine pegged them at "$700 per week" and noted that, on the road, he is trailed by several suitcases of rollers, dyers, relaxers and creams. Equally, the growth in his stature can be measured by an increase in time spent on his hair.

"It's a total ritual, a very central thing," says Gerri Hirshey, who discovered this secret when she hit the road with Brown. "I was shocked, when I first started seeing James, that he would hold court in the middle of it all. I would die, you know, before I would let anyone see *me* in rollers! But, after a while, I was just like everyone else – I'd sit there and make his phone calls for him while he was having it done." Brown has his hair dealt with twice a day, sometimes three times, if he's working – and he conducts much of his business by phone from under the whirring hood of his drier.

Expanding hairstyles have always reflected change in Brown's economic, political and social circumstances. But whatever the orientation of those follicles – and he has moved from slick pompadours and conks to the quadripart "high English" (both back sides and both front sides swept into curves, then blended together) the "processed Afro" and a full bouffant later sidemen secretly term the "*ce*-ment wave" – publically, his 'do is always immaculate. Hair is part of that act of will through which he transcends the other James Brown, the child whose name had passed unnoticed. ("Pronounced," he says, "like one word, 'jamesbrown'.") Hair is central to those rites with which – using speed, action and shape – Brown turned his small, dark self into Mister Excitement.

Brown's childhood friend Leon Austin (then proprietor of Leon's DeSoto Lounge in Augusta) enlightened Gerri Hirshey about just what Brown's transformation meant. "We were talking about why black people were so very enamoured of James," she says. "And Leon, who has also done his hair, said: 'Let me run it down for you. James is dark, he's *ugly*. He made the ugly man pretty because he made himself pretty. But, first of all, that has to do with colour. He made himself pretty *in spite* of bein' dark.' "

In the politics of Brown's showbiz, however, appearance is merely the frame: the suggestive outline of a larger, more existential sacrifice. In front of an audience, Brown becomes a fusion of the preachers who inspired him and the most atavistic, free form American abolitionist. He takes his transformed self, the highest, baddest, hippest character he can construct, and – in a gesture which pierces the crowd to its heart – *destroys* it just for them. In the frenzy of his dancing and pleading, even the most elaborate 'do starts to cascade. And, within minutes, wet curls will be clinging to Brown's face and neck, flopping onto his forehead.

Within seconds, sweat has softened the sharpest lines and creases of his elegant clothing. Eventually, it will fill his shoes, anointing his back and legs. Off come his glittering cuff links (often flung into the audience). Shirt-sleeves hanging, knees stained with blood, James has visibly "given it up" – for the listeners before him in the dark.

This is all part of established African-American performance traditions. Charles Keil, in his book *Urban Blues*, wrote that "the body emphasis, the effort . . . are related to a concept of appropriate and often hyperbolic movements which in turn may dictate a certain style of dress. Cry singers invariably appear in José Greco outfits, removing coat, tie and sometimes the shirt, as their stunts become more strenuous. (This sort of striptease or 'soul baring' symbolizes the idea of getting down to the nitty-gritty.)" But few performers have created a more powerful symbol of throwaway cool – a greater gift to their audience – than James Brown, up there destroying in seconds what it cost him the better part of a day to create.

And, for all its pomp and circumstance, for all its chauvinistic glory, the essence of this practice runs deeper than conventional showbiz glamour and melodrama. Brown's self-demolition is rooted in the backdrop to his tremendous ego and the spectacle it can create – in profound religious beliefs which recognize that, like it or not, all men are meant to be as one. That people are created equal, but just don't *exercise* that thing.

Fred Wesley: "That's something else about James Brown, that particular contradiction. Because contradiction is the very thing which feeds his nerve. He has the nerve to think what he says and does – whether or not he believes it hisself – is going to be taken, perceived as truth. But at the same time, you could hurt his feelings easier than you could hurt a nun's feelings. He is just as fragile as he is tough. Extremely insecure and extremely bold – both at the same time."

Brown himself sticks to the language of performance. "The artist has to *reach*, you know? You come to see my show, you get the atmosphere and the feelin'. And I don't care how well-dressed I am, when I come off, I am drenched in sweat. You know that I was workin' for *you*."

Sweat condenses and epitomizes the alchemy Brown can practice. "When they walk out, my audience knows I gave it for them. That I came on pretty and nice and well-groomed in my tux or my beautiful clothes. And I worked – I worked for them. *Then* I'll go and put on my street clothes, my party things. When I put on my work clothes I come to work. And I make sure my work clothes look good."

Lamé and satin jumpsuits appliquéd with lightning bolts; nineteen-inch flared trousers or spandex drapecoats littered with zips; chiffon neckerchiefs and straw Resistol cowboy hats – to some of Brown's critics through the years, "looking good" has seemed rather relative. "James once had this incredible encrusted thing they called the gorilla suit," marvels Gerri Hirshey, "which weighed an absolute ton and was made by Elvis's tailor at Alamo Clothes – a completely crazy guy in Memphis, who has his wife embalmed in the living room."

In the interests of international understanding, says Briton Cliff White, he has tried to interest Brown in changing style. "I had one lady friend who pointed out that James always looked a lot smarter offstage than on. Offstage he'd wear tailored casuals – he had this one tailored denim suit, for instance, in which he looked really great, quite cool. He'd drive up to the theatre in that – but then he'd appear onstage in outrageous loon pants or a jumpsuit with mile-wide flares. When it's time to start dancing, he puts on a different set of clothes, so he can move around." During the '80s, says White, he tried to convince his friend to adopt "a sort of Little Richard look with short box jackets."

"I was trying to make James understand," he adds, "that if he did a different show in London – with different songs and a different outfit – he would get across much more. Of course, in the same way I can't fully understand his background, he can't really comprehend what the attitude is over here." Despite their resemblance to the uniforms worn by the black bellboys, waiters and train station "Redcaps" of his youth, Brown *did* eventually make the switch to short tailored jackets and matching pants. They stay unwrinkled, he now claims proudly, on even the longest plane journey.

Brown is a practical man – but he believes in epiphany. When he was a pre-teen dancing for dimes in the dust, showbiz did not immediately suggest itself as real economic salvation. But circuses, vaudeville, minstrel shows, barnstorming politicians and tent revivals, he says, filled his early imagination. So did rural evangelists with their theatrical baptisms, fund-drives and conversions. Then, two men's art fused it all – the gospel fervour, the fairground exotica and the music he loved ("I listened to everything round me in those days. Records, jazz, radio, church –

the guy whistling down on the corner.") Men who suggested a syncretism which might embrace all excitements. And, for thirty-five years now, Brown has praised their names: Louis Jordan and Roy Brown.

In terms of both crossover sales and multi-media penetration, jump bluesman Jordan and his Tympany Five stage band became a '40s phenomenon. Brown remembers not just the singer's hits and performances, but also his movies, like '47's *Reet, Petite and Gone* or '48's *Look Out, Sister*. Plus, Jordan worked in Nickelodeon shorts – a sort of early music video tied into the jukebox. Roy Brown, who hailed from New Orleans, was a different sort of star. It was he who wrote – and initially recorded – Elvis Presley's later hit, "Good Rockin' Tonight".

Jordan and Brown were personalities redolent of post-War America, an era when swing carried the beat, and black citizens were stepping out with a newly aggressive assurance. The industrial boom of the war effort had brought blacks more and better jobs, greater purchasing power and – particularly in Los Angeles – more cohesive urban community. LA's Central Avenue (whose thriving music and club scene linked the city's centre to black suburban Watts) helped refine the goodtime dance music audible earlier in the '40s on discs aimed at the black Northeast. This music would become famous as Rhythm 'n' Blues: a sound which shed the nostalgia of the real blues to celebrate black America's exciting, boisterous new moment.

"R'n'B came roaring out of the churches of black America, the black bands of the swing era, and the segregated ghettoes of big cities," wrote Arnold Shaw in his book *Honkers and Shouters*. "Gospel song, heard in storefront, sanctified and shouting churches, gave it intensity and excitement. The black bands contributed the beat and the boogie, and nurtured the singers who became solo artists. The ghettoes created the climate and provided the incentive for young blacks."

To him, says James Brown, Louis Jordan and Roy Brown personified innovation: what a person might *do* with dance music, with the vocabulary of the church-house, with his wardrobe and his emotional history. "Louis Jordan was one of the most dynamic guys ever took to a stage. Ever. He had something you just like to look at. He did movies – and I saw all of those. But I could never get up on movies, cause movies don't let you do reality. That's my thing, reality. What Louis Jordan gave me was a basic concept, a means of communication."

That concept breaks down into several factors. Jordan, for instance, carried a fairly large stage outfit (his Tympany Five would vary between six and eight players). He also paid scrupulous attention to changing fashions – assimilating the jivetalk and social preoccupations of the day into polished, urbane numbers like his "Choo Choo Ch'Boogie" (the 1946 million-seller which clinched his title as the "Father of R'n'B") and "Let The Good Times Roll" ("Don't sit there mumblin' / and talkin' trash / If you want to have a ball / you got to go out and spend some cash / And let the good times roll").

In *The Death of Rhythm and Blues*, critic Nelson George has noted how these songs constituted a "formal marketing strategy" whose crossover aims were both clear and sophisticated: "The titles "Beans and Cornbread", "Saturday Night Fish Fry" and "Ain't Nobody Here But Us Chickens" suggest country life, yet the subject of each is really a city scene. In "Chickens", for instance, the central image is of chickens in a coop having a party that's keeping the farmer from sleeping. But clearly the bird bash is just a metaphor for a black house party that the farmer – perhaps the landlord, maybe the police – wants to quiet. Jordan's vocal, sassy and spirited, spiced with funny, spoken asides, is as buoyant as its shuffling groove. And to an ambitious outsider like the adolescent James Brown, Jordan made one thing intriguingly clear: *cool* could bridge many social gaps which otherwise might seem insurmountable. With cool on his side, a would-be entertainer could overcome pigmentation, poverty, even a ground-zero starting point. Turn his world view – however provincial – into a *style* and even a nobody might become a potent, superbad Self.

"Plus," says Brown, "I knew I could dance."

Conscious of the giant gap between his seat in the stalls and Jordan's graceful command of the stage, James Brown says he never underestimates the effort of maintaining an edge. Quite the contrary, his career has been dogged by bitter criticism of his obsessions: timing, grooming – and RULES. But, Brown explains, when you grow up without such markers, the world is shapeless and formless. *Rules* can generate a world wherein actions are meaningful. *Rules* are necessary when it comes to creative belief.

"Clothes and grooming, for instance. People think that's just everyday. But clothes and grooming mean a *lot.* For me, that's due to the fact that, when I started, I had to borrow shoes to do my dancin' in. When I was little and first wore a suit, I had to wear tennis shoes with it." ("Puttin on a half-pressed suit from the pawn shop with tennis shoes, tryin' to be hip – I know where he's comin' from," rapped Brown on "Mind Power", a track from his 1973 *Payback* LP.)

"But," says James, "At least I'd be *clean.* You look well, your hair's groomed, you try to be respectable. Then you start to get somewhere. And once you get there, it matters even more. Say you bring your mother, your father, your aunt along to see me. You brag on James Brown and you bring 'em to my show and I'm not up there clean and smart." Brown pauses to let the horror sink in. "The good Lord," he notes firmly, "gave me a real role model in Roy Brown. He dressed in suits all the time. And he had a *powerful* vocal style." (Brown says all this with such solemnity it seems that he can *taste* a connection between tailoring and decibels.) "A great strength of volume and a way of shouting I found very unique. Roy Brown was RIGHT ON TOP OF HIS THING!"

Born in New Orleans in 1925, Brown became a vibrant figure in US R'n'B from 1947 – when, after roving Texas and California trying to emulate Bing Crosby, he recorded "Good Rockin' Tonight" for Louisiana's Deluxe Records. But his big success endured only through 1951. James Brown's future label, King Records, bought out his Deluxe contract and, ironically, stalled his career over the five years they kept him. Brown would record successfully again – his self-issued 1978 Faith LP *The Cheapest Price in Town* is one example – but he never really made it back.

Roy Brown invested his tunes – like "Hard Luck Blues", a 1950 R'n'B No 1 – with an incredible morbidity. His mellifluous voice was both chilling and wide in its range; it combined a wide, aching reach with an implicit touch of raw hysteria. The latter quality constantly threatened to subvert the sleazy elegance of his phrasing – and it kept those extreme lyrics in which he specialized ("Got the blues for my baby / I'm down the river serving time / Yes, I shot and killed my baby / Now I just can't keep from cryin'") the right side of self-parody. Even twenty years later, to hear Roy Brown wail a line like "I'm gonna find my mama's grave, fall on the tombstone, and die!" is to feel the chill of life's real weirdness as much as the techniques of melodrama.

It's little wonder Roy Brown appealed to the would-be surrealist in James – his voice could invest even the happiest circumstance with Gothic terrors. An Edgar Allan Poe of the blues, his was the sort of vision to which rural Southern blacks only three generations removed from slavery could certainly relate.

A regard for Roy Brown is part of a politics of region too often downplayed in evaluations of James Brown's work. James is not just "a country person", but a Southern man, a South Carolinian whose trust in his attraction to regional attributes is unquestioning. The emotional expressionism, repetition and spiritual phantasmagoria which surrounded and shaped his earliest perceptions play determining roles in his art. Speaking to Cliff White in 1977, Brown said that his mid '60s masterpieces depended on finally *leaving* the South, and gaining exposure to the cosmopolitan North: "My eyes started opening . . . my brain started to intercept the new ideas and thoughts. I became a big-city thinker. And I started tying that in."

But the determination behind his designs, the glue which held his projects together, resided in an essentially Southern definition of who he was. For black men in the South, survival – a favourite Brown topic – is never a subtle affair. It calls into play high emotions, enormous anger and existential solitude – not to mention mystical concepts about eventual deliverance. The might behind great Southern voices like those of both Roy Brown and James Brown is very real. It is born of a need to shout, to define and to hypnotize, in order to *be*.

Transformed via gospel, blues, and jazz into "soul", this proclamation of self is also rooted in a deep sense of competition.

You can hear it in black lyrical braggadocio and in that audible battle of wills which contributes instrumental intensity to R'n'B. "There was a kind of frenzy and extra-local vulgarity to rhythm and blues that had never been present in older blues forms," wrote LeRoi Jones, now Amiri Baraka, in his classic book *Blues People*. "Suddenly, it was as if a great deal of the Euro-humanist façade Afro-American music had taken on had been washed away by the war. Rhythm and blues singers literally had to shout to be heard above the clanging and strumming of the various electrified instruments and the churning rhythm sections. And, somehow, the louder the instrumental accompaniment and the more harshly screamed the singing, the more expressive the music was." Below the Mason-Dixon line, where the black catchphrase "express yourself" doubles for "speak up – or else", such predilections made perfect sense.

They are part of why James's old pal Bobby Byrd sighs at the very mention of Roy Brown and Louis Jordan: men who defined themselves as blacks, as showmen, as all-American *doers*. At a moment of national change, he senses, these performers managed to get the jump on cool itself. "Roy Brown and Louis Jordan!" says Byrd. "They were our *absolutes*. Louis Jordan, he just *sacked me* when we saw him. Roy Brown, too; from him, in fact, is where we got all that changing of the clothes. He could just upset a house that way; he was changin' twice a show. And what people didn't realize is he was a seamstress, too. Roy Brown *made* his own clothes."

Bobby waits a moment for the import of this to settle in. Then he continues: "It's my belief that everyone gets something from somebody. Blues came out of the church and we took that, made it a little funkier. We caught everyone by surprise when that one drum part changed. When Clyde Stubblefield came on with that funky beat. It was straight out of New Orleans, what his drum was doin' . . . the beats of it was what their conga players do." "New Orleans," he smiles, "*Roy Brown*'s home town."

The man who has hair and teeth and the funk may, indeed, have everything. But if Jordan's cool was the carrot, Roy Brown's miserable solitude was the stick which kept James Brown dancing one step ahead. Never look back, black baseball star Satchel Paige is famous for saying during the '30s, *something might be gaining on you.* It is part of James Brown's funky genius that, through audacity and nerve, he was able to harness fear, machismo and competition – then whip all three into a genre which proselytized for unity and was, in itself, liberation. That he would subsequently succeed in deconstructing this music to expose its most African origins should guarantee him a place in anyone's pantheon of global emancipators.

"I never knew I was makin' that many changes," says Brown today. "No one knew at the time. But I never could let the music change on me; I never could. I had to express myself and bounce back. That dynamic thing of *expressin*' was the strength I saw in Louis Jordan."

grit and guts in a dark decade

"James Brown was like a radio station that picked up on everything: slang, dances, humour. Since disco changed black radio, though, they discourage you from havin' that knowledge and that flair. Now, consultants go out and ask questions, like 'What is it you don't like about your favorite black radio station?' And they take that literally. They say, 'OK jocks – more music, less rap.' But consultants ain't hearin' what people SAY, what the black listener means. It's almost like 'bad' meanin' good. What they really tellin' you is 'this jock ain't saying shit I relate to.'

"James *understood* all that."

Tom Joyner, *Billboard's* Personality
DJ of the Year for 1987, 1988 and 1989

Ten years after he had to masquerade as his drummer just to cut a disc, James Brown was a solo megastar with the tightest show on the road. He was also a musical entrepreneur. Since the early 1960s, he had produced not just his own product, vocal and instrumental, but singles and albums by almost all his female vocalists and groups of sidemen. Some of the records which resulted would achieve massive cult status with fans and collectors twenty years down the line. But, at the time, such projects primarily helped to enhance the aura Brown wanted to build: that of a funky family extolling not just a groove, but the essence of being American and black.

In many of these productions for and with associates, certain themes recur as intrinsic to Brown's ongoing disquisition. Food, "soul food", both literal and metaphysical, is one. Moral responsibilities are another – from Brown's early '60s adjurations to "Think" through the Lyn Collins number of that title ("Think [About It]") he produced in 1972, and Fred Wesley's meditation on preacher Jesse Jackson's "I Am Somebody" litany ("Damn Right I Am Somebody, Parts 1 & 2") in 1974. But *soul* itself is the most dominant. And, in Brown-generated records from Bobby Byrd's "I Know You Got Soul" through Maceo and the Macks' "Soul Power" or Fred Wesley and Charles Bobbitt's "Blessed Blackness", every participant in the James Brown juggernaut contributed their expertise to that great black debate.

Often, soul was the groove, soul was inherent in the instrumental thing itself. From the late '60s to the mid '70s, Brown's omnipotent persona *carried* that swing without which "it" don't mean a thing. And cuts he made possible, such as Pee Wee Ellis's 1969 "In The Middle, Parts 1 & 2" or the JBs' 1970 "The Grunt" – source of a shrieking saxophone which Public Enemy would later use to announce their arrival in hip-hop – enlarged both the lexicon and the unifying instincts of "soul". The *degree* to which Brown accomplished this would not be fully demonstrated for at least fifteen years. But before go-go music, hip-hop, or digital sampling ever emerged, one thing was crystal clear about James Brown and soul. He had taken the existing connotations of truly black music – music rooted in procedures of worship and searches for self that were over 300 years old – and focused them, fused them with *his* moment.

"James had the audacity to believe he could make things happen," says Fred Wesley. "He forced it on people. See, much of what he did, people felt was musically wrong – there was nothing else out there that sounded like this! So he had to *force* people to put it out.

"But he made us all believers," Wesley admits. "Cause every time he'd say, 'It's got that groove, it's got that beat, they can dance to it.' Besides, if I had to fight James Brown, right away I would have a gun. I mean in Round One! Because his determination to win is just uncanny. It's more powerful than anyone else's I've ever seen.

"He has no real musical skills," says Wesley, "yet he could hold his own onstage with any jazz virtuoso – because of his guts. Can you understand that? James Brown cannot play drums at all. But he would sit down on drums and get that look on his face like he's playin' 'em and you would just play along with him. Organ – he cannot play organ at all. A *guitar's* not an instrument you can bullshit on, you got to really know how to play a guitar. And I've seen him pick up a guitar and go #"£#*%*! and look at you just like he's playin' it, you dig?" Wesley roars. "It's incredible. He doesn't understand losing and he truly understands surviving. It's not that James wants to win every time – it's just that he will not lose."

Or, as Brown himself claims he always tells journalists: "*Guts* are what really matters. Guts will take you further than any kind of knowhow." Even the stars, says James, agree – "I'm a double Taurean with a Leo and an Aries. Four strong signs; almost unbelievable."

Guts took Brown to the top – but grits helped, too. Charles Keil once stated that the soul tradition "feeds on truth". And, to his satellites as well as Brown, food was a frequent metaphor in an escalating creative drive. It offered a *frisson* of history, calling up the red beans and rice extolled by Louis Armstrong, the peas and rice and grits and greens and shrimps of the great bluesmen and women – not to mention the fish-fries, beans and cornbread of Louis Jordan's post-War hits. But it reaches back further, too, towards more African definitions of what nutrition is all about: the feeding of the spiritual and cerebral as well as the corporeal self; the satisfaction of the sexual – as well as the racial – identities of man and woman.

It is no accident that one 1972 JBs album was entitled *Food for Thought.* Or that Brown's bands cut numerous tracks with names like "Givin' up Food for Funk" (1972) or "Pass the Peas" – a 1971 meditation embroidered around the simple chant "Pass the peas, like we used to say." Soul's lifeblood could warm the coldest studio if conjured up with the language of a shared dining tradition. Greens, grits, peas – as in the great fountainhead of the blues, the *process* of visceral pleasure (as well as the double-edged demand for "more") permeates Brown's funk. And it unites all sensual pleasures ("For goodness sakes," Brown would intone on a sublimely sleazy disco LP in 1978, "*Take a look at those cakes!*").

"I only interviewed James Brown once," says Afro-American art historian Robert Farris Thompson, "and it was hard to keep track of him, hard to pin him down. But when we moved onto food, suddenly he warmed up. He started talking about the BONE, the ham bone, and the way it *cultures* the greens. Pretty soon, I realised that the food and the sound were going in and out of each other's focus. That, to him, they were things both at one and separate. Both distinct and united."

Much of this metaphor was – had always been – clearly grounded in mundane, everyday realities. Black musicians of Brown's era, as did those before him, travelled, lived and ate in segregated circumstances. Their hotel circuit was, as Thompson puts it, "a chain of floating conservatories – fabulous cells of musical development", where fresh meals and music were always *cooking*, stewing, brewing up. And studio work was the same. "The best stories I got for my book," says Gerri Hirshey, "were all session stories. Because you would be there, in Cleveland or Cincinnati or Nashville, with the writer, the producer and the whole band. You would always be *eating* in the studio, you would be there for hours and hours. The conditions under which work was produced were always either difficult or extreme."

James himself, she adds, was never ready to talk until the earliest a.m. hour – "after he had gone out looking for ribs. No matter where he was, he always had some guy in that town who knew where he could get ribs and chicken at two or three in the morning. He knows every rib joint in the South!"

Popularized in the 1960s, the slang expression "soul food" has now passed into common parlance. And, throughout the American South, soul foods continue to symbolize a basic interconnectedness in black life. Through covered-dish suppers and church socials, fund-raisers and the "Sunday meal" of individual homes and families, this cuisine retains strong links to the sacred. The history it invokes has also begun to receive wider, more "official" recognition. When *The Encyclopaedia of Southern Culture* appeared in 1989, after ten years' work by over 800 scholars, it held that " 'soul food' is in fact the native fare of both black and white Southerners of all economic and social strata", and that "the distinctive ingredients of Southern cuisine, as well as the distinctive styles of cooking them, have been common for centuries in Africa but not in Europe."

The ties between physical refreshment and musical enjoyment, too, are inculcated afresh in each successive generation of Southern African-Americans. During 1977, Virginia writer Susan Hankla conducted poetry workshops in six elementary schools across the state's largely black, economically-depressed Southampton County. The writing Hankla received constantly surprised her, she says, with its vivid perception of life's basics – sound, food, shape and colour – as metaphors for unity. Typical are six lines penned by "Darren" from Southampton's Courtland Elementary: "Love is like eating out / It was like spinach / It was like getting down with turkey / Boogying with the ham / Getting it together with the dressing / Dancing with the jam."

"It *is* like cookin'," says Maceo Parker of the JBs' repertoire. "It's all about spices and attitude towards *dish*! And that is also a regional thing. Even when it's the SAME thing, it's always a little bit different. Because, as a musician, you do stand when you hear your name called, and it's 'OK! North Carolina! Greens, corn, potato pie, OK! Texas tenor – a blast of pepper – wide and open'; fine."

Pee Wee Ellis, who is lunching with Parker at the moment, enthusiastically agrees. "Sure. I *like* more pepper in mine, I lived a long time in Texas. And I remember how, whenever James would play New Orleans, I'd really get excited – mostly about the prawns. Get me some red beans and rice, you know? Me havin' lived so many places, so many different regions and rhythms, I picked up a lot of their flavours. Now I embody all those: Florida's got their thing, Texas got theirs; California's different again."

In 1973, Brown produced Maceo Parker on an track entitled "The Soul of A Black Man". During its intro, Parker – displaying the requisite deference "Mr" Brown always requires – asks James to demonstrate for the listeners "his teachin's": "this thing of what it's like and how it feels and what it's all about." (Soul, of course, though no one needs to actually name the term.) And Brown's great, rough voice reaches across the superimposed, "sweetening" of the strings to cry, "It's so hard! It's so *haaaaaard* . . . When you got three meals a day: oatmeal, no meal : . . and *missed* meal!" This is the purest kind of vernacular poetry, the kind favoured by modern writers from Mayakovsky to Zora Neale Hurston to Sam Shepard – where daily vocabulary, served with a twist, welds collective life and feeling into the artefact of catharsis. (A little further on in the tune, Brown pays tribute to regionalism and its multiple grassroots sympathies as he segues from Parker's powerful solo into a mini roll-call. "Maceo! A man, his horn and his music – and his life . . . I want to send this out to people in Virginia, South Carolina, Florida, Alabama, New York City, New Jersey . . . Texas, Missouri, Kansas, Arkansas, Mississippi, Tennessee; California, Arizona, South Dakota – North Dakota! – Michigan, Ohio . . . *Maceo*! Are you my brother? Come and play us a lil' bit more . . .")

Brown wasn't bluffing with this Rolodex of sites. By the time "The Soul of A Black Man" was cut, he had countless personal and business contacts in every state he names. He had expanded that mystical ability to recruit personnel, to shape his vision, and to "force it" on the world into accurate judgments about something much larger than an audience. By 1970, James had gained control over a whole market. The same year, he cut a stunning consolidation of this ascendancy: a tune called "Get Up, I Feel Like Being a Sex Machine".

The record showcases a brand new set of JBs – including the Collins brothers, "Bootsy" and "Catfish", who would later help to create George Clinton's technofunk utopia, and drummer "Jabo" Starks, who would become as a god to hip-hop samplers then unborn. And it features thermodynamic interplay between Bootsy's bass and his brother's insistent, repetitive licks on guitar. Elastic, expansive and charged, this is funk as an ongoing concern, Brown as a fully-established force in the world of American entertainment. The sound of this pre-eminence would continue through 1975 – with a string of important Brown singles such as "Get Up, Get Into It and Get Involved" (1970), "Hot Pants (She Got To Use What She Got To Get What She Wants)" (1971), "Soul Power, Parts 1 and 2" (1971), "Talkin' Loud and Sayin' Nothing, Parts 1 and 2 (1972)", "King Heroin" (1972), "Get On The Good Foot, Parts 1 and 2" (1972), an exceptional "The Payback" (1974), "My Thang" (1974), "Papa Don't Take No Mess" (1974), "Funky President (People It's Bad)" (1974) – and additional, popular chartmakers like '72's "There It Is, Parts 1 and 2" and "I Got A Bag Of My Own", or '73's "I Got Ants In My Pants", "Sexy, Sexy, Sexy" and "Stone To The Bone, Parts 1 and 2".

In October of 1970, James married a second wife, Deirdre

("Dee Dee"). The same year – as he notes in his autobiography – began with dates in Vegas and ended with a tour of Africa. (There his sound had a seminal effect on the future recordings of Fela Kuti, the Nigerian politician/musician who would fuse the African rhythms of highlife music with the funk of JB to evolve an Afro-pop which has made him famous around the globe.) From May 1971 until 1976, Brown also managed his "People" label, which yielded nine LPs and 50-plus singles. In a feature headlined "Is this the most important black man in America?", he even appeared on the cover of the mainstream US magazine *Look*. (Fear that he might be this powerful, of course, piqued FBI and Internal Revenue Service interest in James Brown –– which, in turn, fuelled his legendary paranoia.)

But by the mid '70s, Brown's world was shifting – bringing changes which would collude to first slow, then almost halt, the singer's amazing creative momentum. For one thing, his incessant, unending demands had begun to take regular tolls of his workforce. Old friends and stalwart colleagues like Bobby Byrd and Maceo Parker started to come and go. There would be three drummers, then two – then one. Bandleader Fred Wesley, who lasted through to 1975 when he defected to join Bootsy and Parker in Parliament/Funkadelic, remembers both sides of that period: the creative as well as the chaotic.

"And I've got to give James credit," says Wesley, "because he allowed me to be creative – he made it possible for me to be ultra-creative. Take a tune like "Doin' It To Death" (in 1973). I would never, ever, in my wildest imagination have thought of doin' something like that. But him givin' me a basic idea caused me to create that. It's my creation, but it's what he gave me to create *with*. He would give you these little, unrelated elements, sometimes not even musical, and say 'make something out of it'.

"Like on 'Good Foot'," he adds. "A horn line like that – NEVER would I think of it. It was just nowhere in my psyche. But this is what James gave me to work with. So now I got to *take* that, and put it along with a silly bass line – what I think is a ridiculous bass line. But you take his little weird elements and put them together into something which *sounds like* something and there you are, changing music."

On a day-to-day basis, however, the James Brown experience continued to be a rough one, with plenty of human fallout. Wesley: "Internally, it was run very weird. You would have to travel long nights and ride the bus; sometimes you wouldn't check into a hotel for three or four days. You did manage to get paid once a week – late usually – but some funny things went on which were distasteful.

"Still," he says, "through the whole thing, when that hit time came, the show was magnificent – absolutely wonderful. It's just that *after* the show you had to deal with James's personality. Where he liked to rehearse and rehearse. And needle and needle, complain and complain. Just generally make life miserable for his bands."

In 1970, Ben "Pop" Bart, Brown's surrogate father and business mentor, passed away. James says it was one of the few times in his life he will admit to crying. Bart's son Jack took over his role, but couldn't practise that old-school, personalized expertise which had made his father such a perfect partner and sounding board for the volatile Brown. Shortly after Bart Senior "passed", something even more ominous occurred: James began getting regular calls and visits from the Internal Revenue Service. His first communication, he says, announced he owed them almost $2 million in back taxes – a sum which was soon "amended" to $4.5 million (just for the years 1969 and 1970). At one point during these tax troubles, Brown was led away from his own home in shackles, "just like a slave". As he served his time in South Carolina's State Park Correctional Center, the Internal Revenue Service still claims he owes the government $9 million in back tax.

Brown's sense of oppression – first from parole restrictions, later from surveillance for his politics and finally, from an unremittingly attentive IRS – is understandable. But, to a background and a psychology like his, it has certainly brought no benefits.

"James *has* made a lot of money," says Cliff White. "Doubtless he squandered a lot of it and the IRS has taken the rest. But most people assume all those guys made a lot of money over the years – when many of them, in fact, were almost starving once the heyday passed. It's a little like the old chitlin circuit theme reasserting itself: 'OK, you can come and play at our club, but you can't eat at the table.' "

James came to realize, says Gerri Hirshey, there were few people he could trust, "and when it came to the government, *nobody*." For despite his endorsement of Humphrey and his early '70s hob-nobbing with Nixon, in terms of the IRS, James Brown was on his own. By the mid '70s, his hard-won acquisitions were disappearing – the radio stations, publishing companies, the buildings, the jet, the Gold Platter Restaurant back at home in Georgia. And the process has never reversed: even the South Carolina ranch-house where Brown's wife Adrienne now resides, awaiting the end of his current sentence, is technically owned by his Georgia lawyer. (Today's James Brown Enterprises office, in an executive park outside Augusta, is also rented property.)

"Anything you talk to him about," says Gerri Hirshey, "whether it's a building, a recording contract, a piece of land, he'll say 'they took it away from me'. 'They took it away' – all the time. He shares some blame for a lot of it, and of that he has no perception at all. But also he got screwed for sure." Little wonder, perhaps, that in July of 1989, State Park Correctional officers discovered Brown was hiding $40,600 in cheques and cash in his prison cell – $40,550 more than an inmate is allowed.

Flash back to the late '50s and '60s, and it's easier to understand that money in the mattress. In those days, the segregated circuit round which Brown's Night Train endlessly steamed was a cash-first proposition – especially if you wanted to keep control of the money you accrued. In 1984's *The Life and Times of Little Richard*, Bobby Byrd recalls being stranded in Georgia with the Famous Flames – and having to ask Little Richard for a loan: "He opened the trunk of his car, reached in and scooped out a handful of dollars without even looking. The trunk of the car was *full* of loose notes of all denominations."

It couldn't have been much of a shock to Byrd. Because, the more Brown & Co learned about the R'n'B "big time", the more clearly they understood the multifaceted functions its cash had to perform. Of course, there was looking good: the front which proclaimed you were *up there* and knew you had to invest. ("I used to come out and make $10,000 a night," Brown says, "but I'd put $11,000 back in, to make my show look good. That's how I thought of it, too. I knew I was paving the way.") But there was another aspect of fully equal importance – the three-way relationship between promotion, progress and the black radio of the time.

In October of 1989, in the airport ballroom of an Augusta, Georgia, Marriott Hotel, something called the "Jack the Rapper Back to the Community Foundation" established America's first Black Radio Hall of Fame. It was named after *Jack the Rapper*, a militant radio tipsheet published from 1976 by well-known black DJ and activist Jack Gibson. Back in October of 1949, Gibson's was the voice initially broadcast by America's first black-owned radio station, Atlanta's WERD. (The first all-black *programming* station in the US was Memphis, Tennessee's WDIA – the "Mother Station of the Negroes" – which went on-air in the autumn of 1948.)

From the '40s through the '80s, Gibson's campaigning to keep black airwaves loyal to their core community has been ceaseless. And The Hall of Fame which memorializes this crusade marks the induction of twenty kindred souls from what trade magazine *Billboard* terms " the golden age of radio" – the pre-1959 period. African-Americans of James Brown's age are likely to remember some of these honorees as "sepia spielers" – "personality DJs" who ruled the airwaves of black radio as it emerged with the late '40s independent labels of R'n'B.

Bebop jocks and jive-talking hep cats, these black personality jocks maximized oral creativity – exploiting the verbal skills of their culture to seize the new potential of radio. In doing so, they sold an awful lot of products to the African-Americans who were listening. Yet they were, as Nelson George has noted in 1988's *The Death of Rhythm and Blues*, trendsetters first and salespeople second. They took a medium where questions of colour could have been evaded (white DJs who trade on black attitudes, slang and style continue to be a staple of radio) and they made it defiantly *black*.

The spielers were aggressively part of the communities to which they broadcast, enjoying expansive relationships with churches, clubs, community organizations, businesses and fraternal bodies. Such jocks could generate fantastic loyalty and, often, local activism. Black personality DJs exploited every new fad and fashion – social as well as musical. And their flamboyant personal histories were quickly bound up with the progress of that music which they played. They served as talent scouts, undertook band recruitment, emceed local dances and contests, functioned as independent promoters. And, of course, they relentlessly plugged and played their musics over the air.

After 1955, with the introduction of playlists and "Top 40" formats, complete control by any radio jock would wither away. But the spielers' brief heyday left both black and white listeners with a powerful legacy: a memory of just how creative (and socially conscious) the airwaves could be. By the time the Hall of Fame had been organized to pay them homage, ten of its twenty inductees had passed on from this life. But the names it honoured (not all, by the way, black) suggest the sort of expressiveness they bequeathed: Oscar "Daddy-Oh" Alexander, Al "The Midnight Gambler" Benson, William "Boy" Brown, Ed "Nassau Daddy" Cook, Mary Dee, Dave Dixon, "Jockey Jack" Gibson, Douglas "Jocko" Henderson, "Joltin' Joe" Howard, Al Jefferson, Paul "Fat Daddy" Johnson, "Chattie Hattie" Leaper, George "Hound Dog" Lorenz, Larry McKinley, Eddie O'Jay, "John R" Richbourg, Rudy "The Deuce" Rutherford, Milton "Butterball" Smith, Jack Walker, and Bill Williams.

The precedents set by these jocks and their fellows during the '40s and '50s went well beyond theory and style. They taught every would-be R'n'B star the art of hustling one-on-one – and the role played by payola. "In the '80s," wrote Nelson George, "it [payola] is still as controversial as it was in the late '50s. But you will never be able to understand its role in black radio . . . unless you realize that most black deejays worked long hours and were grossly underpaid . . . 'Union' was a dirty word. There were no contracts, no health insurance and little opportunity for promotion into management . . . DJs were told regularly that the black janitor could be brought into the studio to replace them at a moment's notice. Their rapid-fire bravado masked economic and social insecurities. They were expected to solicit their own advertising, which encouraged deejays to be hustlers . . . and then management took 90%." (*The Death of Rhythm and Blues*) And so on – and on, up through all the great black deejays who have followed, wrestling to inject personality and communication into those formats and playlists devised by Program Directors, Consultants, "Music Researchers" and Promotions executives.

Twenty years on from the spielers, Alabama-born Thomas Elliott Joyner is modern Afro-America's most prominent "personality" DJ. In 1989, for the third year in a row, he received *Billboard*'s Radio Personality of the Year accolade. Much of Joyner's notoriety stems from the fact that he works two jobs a day – in two major radio markets 2,795 miles apart. From 5.30 am to 9, he is the morning drivetime draw at KKDA-FM in Dallas, Texas, and (after a daily plane flight) from 2 to 6 pm, "Flyjock", the afternoon star at Chicago's WCGI-FM.

Even this jet-setting schedule, however, echoes an earlier precedent: that of superstar spieler Douglas "Jocko" Henderson. "Starting in the late '50s," writes Wes Smith in *The Pied Pipers of Rock and Roll*, "he [Henderson] spent seven years as a commuting deejay, doing a 4-to-6 afternoon show on WDAS in

Philadelphia, then, after a quick meal and a catnap, jumping on a train to New York, where his radio shows were even more of a hit, first on mornings at WLB and then evenings at WADO."

Just like Henderson, Tom Joyner earned his college degree at Alabama's Tuskegee Institute. A childhood pal of pop star Lionel Richie (and lead singer of the original Commodores until his fiancée ordered him to quit), Joyner has been in radio since early 1970. That was the year he first met James Brown – in Montgomery, Alabama – and learned how the personal touch had forged the Godfather's on-air success.

"It had to do with the MCin' of the show," grins Joyner as he relaxes on the sundeck behind his home. "See, whenever he'd come to town, everybody on the radio would meet James after the show. And get a *lecture*, about workin' for the white man, and 'plantation radio'. That lecture would go on about an hour – and James would leave the room. Then his manager would come in, and he'd hand you an envelope. On the envelope would be written your name and 'For MC Services'.

"Who you were," says Joyner, "would determine how much money was inside. But I was just a news guy and there would be twenty to forty dollars in mine! Well, James would do that in every town; everybody at all those radio stations would get a lil' money. And a lecture, always a lecture, about workin' for the white man." Joyner laughs softly. "I think that prob'ly helped him maintain four chart hits a year. Cause everyone at every radio station was his friend. Even if you happened to be just a lowly newsman. But it was more than just handin' you some money, OK? He made an important connection there. And he wouldn't forget, either."

All his associates, past and present, remark upon James Brown's phenomenal memory. ("James just *never forgets*," says

Bobby Byrd, somewhat ominously.) But Joyner considers the singer's facility "absolutely amazing. He just has total recall. Things are happenin' for me now and I'm a big name in my business. But James can remember all the stations where I been before; *he knew me then*.

"And not just me," he adds. "I remember standin' there in 1970, next to a guy named Frankie Stewart. Well, Frankie was an OK jock, been through several stations – but no big markets, nothin' like that. Yet JAMES BROWN knew Frankie, asked him how long ago he left Virginia. And we're in Montgomery, Alabama – this ain't New York City! James knew where that guy had come from – and he had *come from* a town as small as the town we were in."

Brown's obsessive need for control can be counter-productive: it has cost him friends and musicians and the flexibility to adapt when the music business itself has changed. But his insistence on diverting a concert's take into investments like "MC Services" helped to build security for his whole operation. As fabulous as his live act was, Brown suspected no other medium could relate to the black American as broadly or quickly as radio. And he was right.

Tom Joyner: "Sure he was. Even now, time spent listening to the radio by black people in America is much greater than that spent by non-blacks. It's very common to go into a black household where, if they own three or four radios, you'll find all of them on, while the TV is on or even the stereo. Even while they're asleep. Many, many black Americans still sleep with the radio on."

The reason, he adds, has not changed much since the days of the sepia spielers: "What other medium really relates so well to that community? Television? Newspapers? Their images of black people are just nothing like they are in the real world. Anything that does relate to people in the black community, they'll put their arms around it."

Joyner leans forward intently. "And the black community is still not all that diverse, you know? A guy may have lived in the ghetto part of town, then moved to the nicest block. Well, he's still right there in that ghetto – even in that privileged part of town. Cause there's always gonna be people who won't *let* him forget."

Which is something Brown was made to realize, over and over again – first, in the '60s, when he bought a twelve-room palace in Queens from Duke Ellington's former trumpet player; then, in 1970, when he purchased a big house on Walton Way, in the white heart of Augusta, Georgia; and now, on the 62-acre South Carolina spread he no longer owns. Reporting Brown's 1989 trials in the *Village Voice*, journalist Ivan Solotaroff revisited the site of the Augusta whorehouses and gambling parlours young James worked so hard to escape. There he talked with 57-year-old Robert Nunnally, a fellow resident who never made it out of the area, except for a spell in prison. Nunnally told him James still came back "all the time". "Here's where he comes from," he added firmly. "Where his people are. Here on Twiggs, by the bars on Ninth. Not no Walton Way."

With the help of "Pop" Bart, Brown thought he had secured his escape route. Together they built a complex, transcontinental network of radio and retail allies – a human geography which, for many years, virtually guaranteed assiduous airplay and concert promotion for all James Brown product. But, by the end of the '60s, stars like Otis Redding, Aretha Franklin and the Motown roster had amassed a legion of young, white fans. White pop stations started to jump on the new soul releases. And, to compete against outfits with bigger ad-volumes co-opting their material, those stations which served black communities started to change their style. The new aim – which spread across the airwaves of America from New York, where a black jock named Frankie Crocker was "integrating" the formats at influential, black-owned WBLS-FM – was to build a racially-mixed, upwardly mobile audience. And the mellow playlist Crocker pioneered would give America first "disco radio", then, by the 1980s, the "Urban Contemporary" format.

These were the sort of demographics supposed to grab the attention and respect of bigtime national advertisers – as opposed to local, corner-shop concerns. But in the tight, streetwise, fraternal world of US R'n'B, they set off irreversible change. After all, the music which shaped James Brown – as well as the music he went on to create – was made by black artists aiming at black listeners. From *Live at the Apollo* through *Sex Machine*, Brown's work had won a huge white listenership. But Brown's style of control, like "Pop" Bart's brand of management, depended on a system which was personal, regional and accessible on a human scale. And, by 1978, that system had transformed itself, redefined by corporate consolidation and crossover sales.

The '70s became a decade of "Philly Soul" sound – the "message music" of The O'Jays, but also the slicker, upbeat product of Chic, the Three Degrees, and loverman Barry White; a decade of extended dance jams which ended forever the rule of the three-minute pop single; a decade filled with the Jackson Five and their perfect-pop "black bubblegum". It was also a decade of blacks on American movie screens – with soundtrack-spinning "blaxploitation" epics such as '70's *Sweet Sweetback's Badass Song*, '71's *Shaft*, '72's *Superfly* and *Across 110th Street*, even '75's

Mandingo. But, above all, it became the decade of *disco* – a vehicle which engendered the promotion of "white soul" (like that of the Bee Gees) and "Eurodisco" (like that produced by Giorgio Moroder) on black radio stations.

In theory, Brown was already well placed to benefit from most of these changes. By 1971, for instance, the man whose struggles exemplified the pros and cons of the R'n'B indies (and their mirror image in black radio) was himself signed to a corporation. Polydor Records was the US dependant of a European conglomerate – then owned by Holland's NV Philips and West Germany's Siemens AG – to whom Hal Neely (the late Syd Nathan's inheritor at Brown's label, King) had sold all his holdings. Yet even corporate affiliation did not help Brown come to terms with change within the industry.

In his autobiography, Brown blames Polydor almost entirely for his late '70s slump. He cites a dearth of basic creative freedom and lack of sales understanding: "They paid me . . . they paid me more than anybody ever gave me. But they wouldn't give me the freedom Mr Nathan did . . . it was basically a German company, and they didn't understand the American market. They weren't flexible; they couldn't respond to what was happening the way King could." But what had really changed *was* "what was happening".

Again, those changes could have worked in favour of Brown. For years his funk had fought the parameters of the three-minute, 7" single – that's why almost every tune had been released as "Parts 1 and 2" on the same 45. What Brown's circular, extended vamps really needed was that 12" single format brought to prominence by disco (and dominant throughout the '80s via soul hits, rap releases and club remixes). Also, Brown had always slaved to purvey the ultimate in elegant stage showbiz. And elegance, usually taking the form of middlebrow, "Yurrupean" fancification, was another thing the disco age craved. Even with regard to black film soundtracks, James was in from the jump: scoring both Larry Cohen's 1973 *Black Caesar* (aka *The Godfather of Harlem*) and the same year's *Slaughter's Big Rip-Off* – which featured American football great Jim Brown as a Vietnam vet opposing coke-sniffing syndicate men.

Plus, there were the female vocalists. More often than not, the club DJs who drove the disco machine were gay men. They created, then exalted, the so-called "disco divas" of the '70s. Epitomized by Donna Summer, Amanda Lear, Grace Jones, Melba Moore and Gloria Gaynor, such female stars were expected to exude vocal strength – or to personify the *savoir faire* of which suburban discophiles dreamt. James Brown had discovered and recorded fabulous female voices for years – even if most of the ladies concerned contend that their talents were buried beneath Brown's egoistic machismo and emotional terrorism. On his "People" label, Brown pursued this brand of sisterhood right through the disco '70s. And, ironically, cuts like Vicki Anderson's superb "The Message From the Soul Sisters" (pressed under her real name, Myra Barnes) or Lyn "The Female Preacher" Collins' string of recordings – such as '72's "Think", '73's "Take Me Just as I Am" and '75's "Put It on the Line" – speak forthrightly about female dilemmas with which the disco stars merely flirted. Yet, to the influential DJs who manned those disco decks, superficial, overblown kitsch was enough. Real passion posed too much of a threat.

And therein lay the heart of James Brown's whole disco-era dilemma. Reality – his "thing" – was no longer uppermost in the

mind of potential consumers, black or white. As disco progressed
– as it consolidated changes in radio formats, devalued male solo
singers in favour of the iconographic female "diva" and turned
the world of dance music into a digitalized producer's medium –
there was a flight from that gritty, basic, everyday universe which
supplied his art. Even among Brown's core audience, disco
opened a generation gap. Artists such as Chic, Donna Summer,
David Bowie, Deniece Williams, the Stylistics and the [Detroit]
Spinners were redefining cool for young blacks as well as young
whites. And that cool was far from the processed pompadours (or
soul brother Afro) and matching suits (or dashiki) of previous
days. Their idea of showbiz sex and glamour was epitomized in
Donna Summer's robotically orgasmic, eight-minute, 1976 smash,
"Love to Love You Baby". Disco promoted irony over honesty. It
offered sexual theatre rather than soulful entertainment.

Integrated crossover hits of the early '70s, like those by KC and
the Sunshine Band (fronted by white soulboy Harry Casey, who
worked out of Florida studios owned by Henry Stone, the man
who helped JB record his band as "the Swans") demonstrated
that disco's groove had originated in Jamesian funk. But disco
became a desert for Brown: he couldn't determine a path and he
couldn't manage a stylistic *coup*. Reality, it seemed, had turned
from an ally into an enemy. First there had been Pop's death, then
IRS persecution, and then – in June of 1973 – came the accidental
loss of his firstborn, Teddy Brown, in an automobile wreck. He
couldn't cry at the funeral, says Brown. But friends recall how he
got up and ran out of the church.

Sadly, there was nowhere to run. In 1976, a Newark, New Jersey,
US District Court launched its own investigation into payola and
black radio. And Brown associate Charles Bobbitt, the singer's

former manager, told them he had passed Frankie Crocker nearly $7,000 to have the Godfather's records played. Under oath, Brown denied the charge. And, although others were fined, Crocker was never convicted. But Brown's public image, as well as that of black radio, certainly suffered.

At the same time, even Brown's role as chief funkateer was being challenged – by musicians he had lost, recruited as crusaders for George Clinton's epic, polyrhythmic dance projects. A satirical, high-tech funkologist (and therefore equipped to battle disco through the final, digital ditch), Clinton had spread his utopian groove through a dizzy array of ensembles: centrally, Parliament and Funkadelic, with satellites such as Bootsy's Rubber Band (a vehicle for Brown ex Bootsy Collins), the Horny Horns (stuffed with JB alumni), Parlet and the Brides of Funkenstein. Clinton himself saw this expansive, wild-card creativity – typified by '70s titles like "Free Your Ass and Your Mind Will Follow", "Maggot Brain", "America Eats Its Young", or "Standing on the Verge of Getting It On" (a perfect description of the tensions milked by JB's classic funk) – as only the latest instalment in a politically-conscious black dance continuum. From Sly Stone to Jimi Hendrix to George Clinton, he reasoned. But all, and only, standing in the shadow of James Brown.

The line of descent was clear enough – and so were the ties of form. Clinton's muse, for instance, was explicitly political. It depended on black street slang, fads and fashions. And it was realized most fully as live, theatrical event, onstage. (Disco radio didn't give George much airplay either, his work was too sprawling, too "raggedy", and too black.) But Clinton's shows were legendary and his records soon became a cult. He caught the pulse of a black America still not entirely convinced by disco –

and Clinton took Brown's groove places Brown himself could not.

Fred Wesley defected from Brown to Clinton and Co in 1976. "I was just fed up," he recalls. "And also, it just seemed like a natural progression. Bootsy and George are people I put at the top of any creative list, right? But what made the real difference was the way they put it to me. Like: 'Bootsy's doin' the rhythm thing, George is producing, does words and concepts – we need you to do horns.'

"When I first talked to George I said, 'Well, what type of horns do you want?' And he said, 'I'm not going to tell you what to do – I want YOU. I want Fred Wesley to do me some horns.' " Wesley shakes his head. "I thought – THIS sounds different! Because with James Brown the things that I'm known for are things he influenced me to do. When I went with George and Bootsy, the only thing that influenced me was their creativity. It was always MY horn lines, MY horn licks – *my* creativity."

During the early years of disco, there was still plenty of James Brown to be heard: from 1970 to 1975, he had nine R'n'B No 1 records, eighteen Top 40 pop singles, a third *Live at the Apollo* LP (*Revolution of the Mind*), 1972's "message rap" "King Heroin" – and two important albums, released in '73 and '74: *Hell* and *The Payback*. Plus, Polydor was churning out the JB re-releases; under titles like '72's *Soul Classics* and '73's *Soul Classics Volume II*. But, still, the decade ended with Brown billing himself as "The Original Disco Man". And at his shows he was sporting defensive slogans like "I'm Black – I'm Back!" or "The Man Who Never Went Away".

Cliff White attributes much of Brown's '70s struggle to bad production advice – and a certain loss of nerve in the face of creative stress. "You notice he hasn't *really* made a decent record in a decade," says White, "and he hasn't produced himself for about a decade, either. Trouble was, in the late '70s when his career began to fall apart, he kind of lost his sense of direction.

"When he was feeling, 'Well, I'm doing it – everything I put out is a smash,' and just acting spontaneously, then the music was great. And it *was* a hit most of the time. As soon as he started to feel, 'What's happening, I'm not getting hits any more,' it became 'Well, maybe I oughta bring someone else in to do this, do that.' "

Tom Joyner feels it was less lost spontaneity than cold business considerations. "The disco thing took over, man, it changed the whole ball game! And when radio altered to a more formatted, researched kind of thing, then his way of gettin' over with records just wouldn't work no more. James made his thing in a day when you didn't have Program Directors and Research Consultants – you had hustlers. The music was as free-feel as the radio was, it was all the same."

Whatever the specific roadblocks Brown encountered, the *music* of the '70s remained indisputably Jamesian. "Pervasive as Brown's influence was in the '60s," wrote Robert Palmer in *Rolling Stone's History of Rock*, "he has shaped the music of the '70s even more profoundly. The chattering choke rhythm guitars, broken bass patterns, explosive horn bursts, one-chord drones, and evangelical vocal discourses he introduced . . . have become the *lingua franca* of contemporary black pop, the heartbeat of the discothèques, and a primary ingredient in such far-flung musical syntheses as Jamaican reggae and Nigerian Afro-beat."

Plus, in 1974, Brown produced a song called "The Payback" – as seminal a piece, in its way, as his 1965 "Papa's Got a Brand New Bag". Poetically explicit, this is a call for reparation, a demand that white America honour its economic and spiritual debts to the

African-American. Set within a deep, ominously bubbling funk, its language is specific:

> "Got to – got to / Payback – REVENGE! / I'm mad – gotta get back, I need some get back / PAYBACK, PAYBACK / like this – PAYBACK – revenge – I'm mad / You get down with my girlfriends – that ain't right / Whoooaaa – talkin'. . Payback is a thing you got to see / Hell! You never do any damn thing to me / Sold me out / For chicken change (yes you did) / Tol' me you—they—had it all arranged / You hand me down and that's a fact / Now, punk, you gotta get ready / For the big payback! / I can do wheelin' / I can do dealin' / But I don't do no damn squealin' / I can dig rappin' / I'm ready – I can dig scrappin' / But I can't dig that backstabbin' (oh no) / My brother get ready (that's a fact) / Get ready, mother – for the big payback / Took my money, y'got my honey / Don't want me / To see / What you're doin' to me / I can get back / Gotta deal with you, gotta deal with you / I – gotta – deal with you / Lemme tell you."

On the original 7″ version a stage MC interjects talkover dedications ("This record is for – *Los Angeles*! ... This record is for ... EVERYBODY!") and boasts ("This record is .... STONE!"). But it was history – both immediate history and the American Reconstruction era of 1865–1877 – which gave "The Payback" a double whammy of resonance.

As far back as the '60s, James Brown's work explicitly anticipated many questions which would dominate the cultural debates of the '80s: the legitimacy and importance of "black" English, the role to be played by black capitalism and the need to reconsider educational Eurocentricity. And the issue of reparation raised in "The Payback" is the same one which animates those late '80s African-American reparations bills constructed by US legislators like William Owens (a Massachusetts state senator) and Representative John Conyers of Michigan. "Although the demand for reparations has acquired a radical tinge," *In These Times* reporter Salim Muwakkil reminded his readers, when he wrote on such legislation in October, 1989, "the idea is nothing new. During the Reconstruction era, Congress heatedly debated but ultimately defeated the proposal to award freed slaves '40 acres and a mule'. Even ardent segregationalists understood the cruel injustice of setting slaves free without the means to survive. Freedom was a perilous thing for those who had been prohibited from learning to read or otherwise acquainting themselves with the customs and culture of the people who once enslaved and still despise them." Nor does the idea of financial repayment as a requirement of racial justice seem likely to disappear. In March of 1990, Minister Louis Farrakhan, controversial President of America's 10,000-strong Nation of Islam, chose to link his call for black separatism to fresh reparation demands. "Since we built this country," *The Washington Post* quoted the 56-year-old NOI leader as saying, "give us reparations . . . give us what you owe us."

Those with a modern interest in the issue of reparation would do well to check out the 1973 sleeve of Brown's *The Payback*. (From *Sex Machine Today*, with its title spelled out by a Kama Sutra of lissome, naked women, through the bleak ghetto cartoons which cover the double LP *Hell*, one might devote a book to Brown's album covers alone.) Its front cover combines African-American lovers with an exchange of money and a vision of the Tree of Life – visual "thoughts" of that behatted James

Brown whose portrait dominates the painting by Don Brautigan. Inside, the reference is even more specific: on a tractor, in an Impressionistic haze of sunlight, an African-American farmer plows his field. "It all began with forty acres and a mule," read liner notes by Brown's road manager Alan Leeds. "A simple desire . . . but nothing good is simple."

These lines repeat on the back sleeve, this time as a hymn to that "Mind Power" celebrated by the album's closing track. "IT'S TIME FOR PAYBACK," the notes declare, "AND PAYBACK IS GONNA BE A MUTHA!!"

Other factors make the song itself sting. One of the strongest is Brown's very personal anger and frustration – the specific stress and claustrophobia he was starting to feel from the '70s. ("Gotta get those *hits*," he raps in another section of the song.) In these emotions, wounded machismo plays its part. But equally provocative was the contemporary meaning accrued by the term "payback" at the time of the song's release – as used by returning Vietnam vets, many of whom were black.

"Payback" was always slang for getting return on what you put in. Getting what you deserve. But to vets in the early '70s, "payback" had become an ironic term, permeated by the violence and mockeries of the War. Its meaning was as bitter and twisted as their experience of Uncle Sam and combat itself. And, because they were doubly invisible, black vets were doubly troubled. Ignored as men in their own country – yet sent to do a "man's job", often in place of their white counterparts – African-American vets returned home to find US society embarrassed by their very existence. Marginalized by both America's mainstream and its "counterculture", the black Vietnam veteran epitomized African-American machismo as rage. And, as the War wound to its dismal close, James Brown gave those years of bottled-up anger and destruction a slogan – the cry of righteous demand. *Payback*. Every black listener understood that his "I gotta deal with you" lyric was a code for "You *gonna* deal with me".

The demands of Brown's 1974 No 1 (on the R'n'B chart, of course; pop-wise it went to 26) were, then, both venerable and contemporary. But its true message is more global than American.

And that is because something far deeper than a common descent from Mother Africa, or the desire for a culture of African derivation, continues to unite the dispersed black peoples of the globe – the "diaspora". That something is a shared set of moral passions, the legacy of Africa's ancient religious and philosophical systems. These passions which span the world, transcending many kinds of secondary or imposed languages and cultures, are not easily articulated. But they can be immediately *apprehended* – and, in the work of James Brown, they have been perceived and acknowledged from Georgia to Zaire, Mexico to Jamaica.

Action, not articulation, lies at the heart of this shared identity. Action and reaction (*repetition*), balance and equilibrium (*cool*), giving and receiving (*payback!*). Across the diaspora, kindred elements of art embody the whole round of human existence on this planet as it is understood – and made sense of – by the world's oldest cosmologies. Brown's music has always given their kinship both a voice and a vehicle. And that is what makes him an icon who remains both eternally "modern" and thoroughly universal. The kind of idol whose meaning will always transcend his "standing", his sales and the who-played-what-on-which-record which also constitute his work.

That name – *jamesbrown* – which had once been a symbol of failure and exclusion was, by the end of the '70s, a code for black and proud, a talisman of magic dimensions. When, in 1977, a six-year-old African-American student at Virginia's Boykins Elementary School wanted to write a poem for his mother – whom he called Hattie King Grape – he invoked Brown's power as a birthright:

> *Hattie King Grape*
> She is on the t.v. saying how the color comes out of her children's clothes She said that her daughter has a blue dress and it turn white and she had a blue pair jeans and they turn white.
> She say she might have to put some James Brown powder into it.
> So when the children went to school singapore pink was in their clothes, and it didn't fade white instead it turn frog green and bug black
> *the end*

As Robert Farris Thompson puts it, "the culture Brown embodies is above and beyond politics, in the sense that its black triumph is inevitable. That's the message from James Brown just as, today, that's the message of hip-hop. When a black car rolls down the street of any city in the world with *doom doom BWAH.* blaring from every orifice, that's what it's saying. It's like a banner unfurled.

"This is a culture on the go," he adds. "Who *else* is creating all of this dynamism for us to dance to? To become encouraged by? They kept us hale and healthy for twenty years, and got us through World War II. The black people of the world keep bailing us out. But for how many decades can they bail us out of our psychoses before it's pay-up time?

"The doctor's bills are *due*," says Thompson. "In the '90s, in the 21st century, you'll have incredible black political triumphs. And, somehow, James Brown is right in the middle of it all."

Payback.

minister señor love daddy

"We need a balanced religion. Religion is not either/or; it is both/and."

Ward African Methodist Episcopal Church Annual Report, 1983-1984 Ward A.M.E., Los Angeles, California

"If you knew about Toccoa, where we started at," says Bobby Byrd, "you'd know *everything* was church – still is. Church is what there is to DO."

When James Brown transformed Bobby Byrd's sextet – catalyzing a set of hobbyists into the vehicle for his gargantuan ambitions – it was God and his Gospels which gave him the tools. God in the form of that Southern black American church which carries encoded within its practice the worlds of ancient Africa. From its pulpit, its pews, its rhythms, its preoccupations and the spectacular "stylin' out" of its preaching fraternity, came the Minister of the New New Super Heavy Funk – a man who can rightfully claim to have used "the auditorium, the boat, the stadium and the jukebox for my church."

Compared to the enterprise and magnetism of the African-American religion which governed Brown's earliest interpretation of life, the style of Louis Jordan, the mighty larynx of Roy Brown, even the blasphemous ecstasies of Little Richard are as nothing. Only with some understanding of that church and the resonance of its rituals, can Brown's stylized world – as well as his impulse to fabricate it in the first place – be understood. For when James Brown speaks about his funk, he is talking also of epiphany and revelation: the transmogrification of life through rhythm and allusion. He's talking about alchemizing that Carolina dirt on which he walked into a shining, white pathway that leads to a place of eternal safety and perfect equilibrium.

In the low Carolinas and small-town Georgia of James Brown's childhood, every black child came to consciousness surrounded by religious talismans of hope. Everyday black life might demonstrate little cause for optimism. But the church which encircled the African-American community charged it with a profound belief that all things are to be changed. Throughout the South, black graveyards translate the preached and sung philosophies of that Afrocentric church into concrete imagery of a deep spiritual continuum.

There, jars of white chicken feathers honour the purified spirits of the departed (and protect them from evil). Sea shells indicate the ebb and flow of human life: from daily travail to eventual glory; glass bottles and shining tinfoil tremble with the brilliance and deceptive strength of the soul. The great legacies of Africa are everywhere: in song, in custom, in preaching style and sentiment, in commonly-held black Southern ideas about what it means to "endure".

Within church walls – the starting point for James Brown's music – this inheritance finds its focus in the preacher and the gospel soloist. But, consonant with the message of redemption, performance in the black church also strives to include the least member of a congregation.

"There are two basic sources from which gospel singing has derived its aesthetic ideals," writes Pearl Williams-Jones, a member of the music faculty at Washington DC's City College. "The freestyle collective improvisations of the black church congregation and the rhetorical solo style of the black gospel preacher. . . The same techniques are used by the preacher and the singer – the singer perhaps being considered the lyrical extension of the rhythmically rhetorical style of the preacher. Inherent in this also is the concept of black rhetoric, folk expressions, bodily movement, charismatic energy, cadence, tonal range and timbre . . . The gospel experience is almost ritualistic in its sustained drama and spiritual intensity."

This theatrical experience of the Gospels is not to be found at

every black American church. But it flourishes in those rural folk
churches which cover the South, in the region's fundamentalist
institutions (whether Baptist or Methodist, Presbyterian or
Episcopal) and their "storefront" counterparts in the urban
North. Across America, the 1980s have also witnessed a rebirth of
proudly black African Methodist Episcopal congregations. (The
"AME" church, a stronghold of African preference and custom,
came out of Pennsylvania's Free Africa Society – worshippers
headed by a former slave who became a clergyman – in 1816.)

Much of the black gospel worship experience would sound or
look immediately familiar to James Brown concert-goers and fans
who might never have set foot in any such church. For instance:
deacons who rush to throw successive mufflers or wraps around
an agitated preacher while he paces behind the pulpit, stopping
periodically to admonish his parishioners. Listeners who vocally
participate in his *extempore* creation of a sermon. Or the soloist
who "worries" the line he or she sings, wringing from each word
and change every possible drop of emotion. Not to mention that
singer who "builds" on the impact or sentiment of a rendition by
repeating key words over and over.

Funk fans will also be familiar with Brown's characteristic
interpolation of "HA!" into all sorts of vocal proceedings. 1969's
recording of "Let A Man Come In And Do The Popcorn, Parts 1
and 2" provides a good example, in a rumination that runs:
"Waaaay over yonder can you / Dig that mess – HA! / Sister standin'
out there, HA! / Dressed up / In a brand-new mini-dress / Look /
Hey! Over there / Do you see that boy – HA! – playin' that horn? /
And get back – HA! – that soul brother / look at him doin' that /
Popcorn – UH!"

For an explanation of this phenomenon, one can look as far

back as the pre-1948 writings of black folklorist and pioneer sociologist Zora Neale Hurston. In her famous essay "The Sanctified Church" Hurston notes that: "The well-known HA! of the Negro preacher is a breathing device. It is the tail end of the expulsion just before inhalation. Instead of permitting the breath to drain out, when the wind gets too low for words, the remnant is expelled violently. Example: (inhalation) 'And oh!', (full breath) 'my Father and my wonder-working God', (explosive exhalation) 'ha!'."

Listeners, critics and Caucasian parents also remark on Brown's constant, circular use of repetition. Legend has it that even King supremo Syd Nathan opposed the initial recording and distribution of "Please Please Please" since he simply couldn't understand a three-minute song with "just one word in it". And sixteen years later, Brown's habits had not changed. In Brown's 1972 "Get on the Good Foot", rock critic Robert Christgau noted: "lines repeat from song to song – 'The long-haired hippies and the Afro-blacks / All get together off behind the tracks / And they party' – and so do riffs. The hook on the 12-minute "Please Please" (not to be confused of course with "Please Please Please") repeats 148 (and a half) times."

Brown's repetition and circularity – clearly transferred from sacred to secular musics and performance – are something much larger than a personal eccentricity. They denote a black culture with Afrocentric values, values distinctly separate from white European systems of thought about the physical world.

James A Snead stresses how, in black culture, repetition means that a thing circulates "in an equilibrium": "In European culture, repetition must be seen to be not just circulation and flow but accumulation and growth. In black culture, the thing (the ritual, the dance, the beat) is 'there for you to pick it up when you come back to get it'. If there is a goal . . . it is always deferred; it continually 'cuts' back to the start, in the musical meaning of 'cut' as an abrupt, seemingly unmotivated break . . . with a series already in progress and a willed return to a prior series."

The Afrocentric world view to which repetitions like James Brown's allude, then, consciously or as received patterns, is not one of linear progression. It is far earthier, far more prescient. This is an apprehension of the universe as present-tense yet balanced: a world at peace within its natural rhythms and cycles.

Which leads to the thing European "post-modern" minds find hardest to grasp about most profoundly sacred systems of thought . . . that such worlds can be at peace with natural change — or unexpected calamity – because their belief embraces both. The profane as well as the sacred, the good as well as the bad, the accidental as well as the logically-foreseen occurrence hold equal force in such cosmologies. And in black American culture, thanks to the Afrocentric base of that church which shaped its perceptions, Saturday night is only the "other half" of Sunday morning. A resignation pervades the art and song and speech of the certain black South, just as a certain simplicity unifies them. For black Southern history is not remote, something left behind by the march of "progress". It is experience – constantly revealed, re-lived, and re-interpreted in terms of the fresh, contemporary moment.

As James Brown's adaptations of gospel music, his own brand of preaching, and the moral admonitions of his music demonstrate, these are not static but *dynamic* belief and performance traditions. Improvisation and innovation are expected. In *I Got The Word In Me And I Can Sing It, You Know*, his book on the performed art of the African-American sermon, Gerald L Davis makes the point that "however African-American performance and creativity might be observed, the organizing principle of circularity, rather than linearity, is evident . . . it holds a central, core importance in African-American performance."

Whether one calls this "roots" or "the groove", such an "organizing principle" is easily seen onstage in the acts of Brown, Clinton, Prince or a jazz ensemble. Across the diaspora, listeners may apprehend its heartbeat in recurring musical phrases or in slices of common slang which turn up again and again. It is palpable in the impulse of a black graffiti artist to "tag" a wall and in the care with which a young jazz dancer will re-interpret a step from the 1930s. For in the Afrocentric universe of rhythmic, poetic unities, what goes around comes around. Everything has a place and everyone will have their time. "Hold On – I'm COMIN'". "Yes, I AM SOMEBODY". "BOOMSHAKALAKA!" . . . *Payback*.

Even the young rappers and hip-hop breakdancers of the '80s, whose work is founded on the Jamesian beat, sense this history behind their art – not to mention Brown's central role as a conduit of that history. Rap artist and producer Afrika Bambaataa is explicit: "Things always go in cycles, you see. Even when James is talkin' onstage it might have been a whole lot of different components. But they were all round and in rhythm. 'Hey fellas – YEAH – Oh Fred, Oh Ma-ce-o – *Hey*! Gimme some more!' Like that. That orientation played a big role in a lot of later groups.

"And it all," maintains Bambaataa, "it *all* translates back to Africa. That's why I took my name – although, in truth of the word, 'Africa' was just the name an Italian gave to the continent. I was among the first to start tellin' people rap goes all the way back to Mother Africa, and I was tryin' to show them through James. It goes back through his call-and-response – which is also the

church – through even the poetry of Gil Scott-Heron and Nikki
Giovanni, through the sayin's of Jesse Jackson and Malcolm X and
Minister Louis Farrakhan. Through politicians when they start
talking jive or the dozens you play where it's 'your mama does
blah blah, your sister does it too' – you STILL RAPPIN' there. Through
(*Dewey*) Pigmeat Markham's old vaudeville act 'Here Come De
Judge' or the lovesexy talk of Barry White. Or Isaac Hayes or the
nasty ole love-type get-it-back-on-ya Millie Jackson stuff. ALL this
kinda thing: it's AFRICA.

"James, he showed us all that," says Bambaataa. "Basically,
James gonna live forever. Even when he goes, he gonna keep on
ministerin'. Gonna be generation 'pon generation up until the
Space Age, still groovin' to James Brown moves."

James Snead describes the bloodline of James Brown's art as an
essentially "social" rhythm: the Afrocentric beat, he says, is "an
entity of relation". In other words, it is rhythm whose expectations of change, of improvisation, surprise and participation are
deeply embedded. And, from the interplay of successive JBs
through those jokes Brown trades with viewers and listeners,
rhythmic "participation" also symbolizes black spiritual unity.
This is another legacy of the Mother continent. Musician John
Miller Chernoff, in his 1979 *African Rhythm and Sensibility*,
describes such enactments of communally-apprehended spiritual
values as "perhaps the most fundamental aesthetic in Africa:
without participation, there is no meaning. To an Accra [Ghana]
'guy'," says Miller, "James Brown's lyrics in particular are 'thick
with proverbs' comparable to the most philosophical [Ghanaian]
highlife songs . . . Many of my [African] friends were eager for my
help in translating James Brown's slang, which they interpreted
with no end of enjoyment and wonder."

Week after week, the spiritual force of collective artistry is made manifest in the black Southern church – and in African-American churches throughout the United States. And at its centre stands the preacher himself. Charged to speak in language comprehensible to his least-educated listener (and expected to make clear reference to the daily events and temptations of life), it is little wonder Amiri Baraka recently termed the black preacher "our first warrior, our first guerrilla".

Sociological discussions of black preaching and its art make much of what black congregations anticipate: a grand use of rhythm and melody; arousing drama and vivid metaphors; and a quick response to ongoing audience interjections (such as "thank the Lord!"; "I *hear you*!"; "Tell us, brother!", etc). And, at its best – as white America learns when it views the Reverend Jesse Jackson or film of Martin Luther King – black American preaching will fuse text and style so as to transcend class or regional differences. Its focus will be on emotion – the tool which will implant the preacher's moral objectives most deeply.

From those churches where young James Brown sought excitement, security and income (he relied on Sunday crowds for regular shoe-shine earnings), he also absorbed crowd dynamics, a wealth of musical inspirations, stylistic and performance models. Paramount among the latter is a preaching skill still known colloquially as "stylin' out". Here speech professor Grace Sims Holt (like Brown, a South Carolinian) describes that basic black pastoral imperative:

> Whatever other functions fell to the minister in the early black church, it was clear that the most important one was to create a form of hallucination that would provide the

basis of hope which would allow one to endure another week, at which time emotional release could again be provided. It was in the capacity to arouse an emotional response that these ministers became true artists; none lacking this talent can survive in the black church. The rich, descriptive, allegorical phrases in black English are paraded before the congregation, and the response of the church is emotionally charged with sisters fainting, sweating, groaning and simulating a mass orgasm. The service itself is as formal, rigid and stylized as a Catholic mass, but unlike the mass – which is designed to be remote, mystical, solemn – the *raison d'être* here is emotion. The frustrations of living the black life are vented in paying homage to the white God (more recently, the black God).

The emotional charge of which Holt writes comes from "gettin' happy" – leaving the fears of everyday life for a moment of ecstasy which mirrors one's eternal salvation and actualizes the transformation with screams, shouts or fainting fits. With verbal as well as physical interjections, the congregation responsively completes the litany of their preacher. Such black church rituals confirm the sophistication of their African antecedents. For, if those religions had not embodied a consummate responsiveness to drastic changes as well as everyday life, displaced slaves would never have found it possible to worship the same white God as their tormentors. Yet they took the white man's religion and, as Holt quotes Reverend Calvin Marshall saying in a 1970 issue of *Time*, "We made it work for us in ways it never worked for him."

James Brown credits all his work to the God of that ultra-resourceful, pragmatic, Afro-descended church. "Where do good ideas come from?" he demanded to know when radio journalist Christina Patoski queried his gospel roots. "They have to come from a good spirit. That seems to me to mean they come from God. Yep." His voice resonates with case-closed finality.

"My music is like a parable," he says today. "When you get happy, you don't quite get enough. An' you just keep doin' it and doin' it and – it's the way people react when they get happy in church. Really I've always gone for that same kind of spiritual concept. Preachers did inspire me: Brother Joe May, Daddy Grace, Rev C L Franklin, Aretha's daddy. And Little Richard, of course.

"They taught me," says James, "that you let people be themselves and *see* themselves in your work. Cause everyone can't run a computer, be a big basketball player, be the best. Everyone can't get an elevation. So I went for person-to-person contact, lettin' the people realize you are there to lift 'em up. To me that IS the live element – and that came from my church."

Ask him about explicit connections with Africa and Brown grows slightly uneasy. ("I went over there and I heard their thing, and I felt their thing. But I honestly hadn't heard their thing in mine.") It's as if he fears a compromise of his personal Southern Christianity.

"Before my interview with James Brown began," says Robert Farris Thompson, "He suddenly interjected: 'Dear LORD! There is a man here presuming to interview me. Pray IN THY NAME it goes well. Pray that he not disgrace me and the work of my people. Pray that he will honour me – IN THY NAME I ask, AMEN! Now ... *First question?*'

"I know Brown thinks his African-ness could be a problem," adds Thompson. "He feels that, to admit it, he might have to give up his religion. But in the 1990s, misapprehensions like that will disappear. People are going to realize that to be a Baptist or an African Methodist Episcopalian in black America is automatically at the same time to have been practising, coded and creolized, the classical religions of the Kongo.

"Europeans – English Anglo-Saxons and blue-eyed whites – for instance, say 'God'. But black Americans say 'Great God A'Mighty'. 'Great God A'Mighty' is a translation of *Nzambi Mpungu*: the greatest, highest form of God – the monotheistic whammy in the sky!

"James Brown," Thompson says firmly, "is already *there*, he was already blended. There is nothing here for him to lose. The Bakongo themselves welcomed the Catholic fathers and took on the cross of Jesus – because they saw similar, equal potency. So that is the cry of the future: the cry of the blues and the cry of James Brown and the cry of the whole Afro-Atlantic world! To stop seeing each other as problems and realize these are *equal* potencies."

Those vocal traits Brown apprehended from the preachers, R'n'B belters and bluesmen of his youth had been preserved by the spirituals and, later, by gospel tradition. They culminate in his titanic, freeform scream: the Oooohhoooohh! Aaaaaaaooooooow and Wheeeeeeooooooooh and WhaaaaAAAAAAAH which have perplexed Caucasian listeners since he first recorded in 1956.

"Whites don't realize what that scream is," confesses Robert Farris Thompson. "They don't understand that it's a code, that it is another language. That we are not just 'black' – we are *multiply* black. In that sense, James Brown is more African than the Africans! In his funk and his vocal quality – those growls, those slurs – you hear real central African stuff: textless displays of verbal energy, as in yodel sounds and screeches and cries. He's kept to that completely. Things which were filtered from Africa around the Caribbean and throughout the Mississippi Delta, he refiltered those things from the church into our consciousness.

"Even the electric boogie, the breakdancers' original move," says Thompson, "came out of the African-American church. It started with that primordial jerking of the spirit in the shoulder blades. You just needed to add a little robotic motion."

Thompson has written for years on African and African-American dance, music and visual art as religious faith: as practices which habitually, daily, fuse the sacred with the profane.

James Brown puts this fusion another way when, in 1972's thumpin', bumpin', wailin' "Funky President (People It's Bad)", he interrupts a political message ("Let's get together, get some land / Raise our food like the Man / Save our money like the Mob / Put up a factory on the job!") to emit a tremendous shriek and cry, "Hang on! Turn on your funk motor and get down and praise the Lord! / Get *sexy sexy* – get funky and *dancin'* / Love me baby, love me twice't / Don't make it once but can you make it twice't – I like it!" He goes on to incorporate both business advice and boogie into a single text: "Turn up your funk motor, I know it's tough! / Turn up your funk motor, 'til you get enough – yeah / Hey, give yourself a chance to come through, *whoooo*! / Tell yourself: I can do what *you* can do."

Thompson is the exceptional Anglo-European critic and not merely with respect to his lifetime of primary-source research. No, the character of Afrocentric soul religion makes many white folks uncomfortable. For some, it seems too untrammelled, *too* emotional. Others find Africa's cosmic unities overwhelming – they prefer that classical ignorance which terms these extremes of clarity "primitivism". Or else, for alienated, 20th-century minds primed to dissect rather than to apprehend, Afrocentric expression is just too confusing.

Take just one example: James Brown's rapid-fire thematic "cuts" – his abrupt shifts from a chilling scream to a sensual come-on, from a rousing political slogan to an especially sleazy "HEH-HEH-HEH". To many Caucasian listeners, these are bizarre non-sequiturs no less schizophrenic than the moment, back in 1966, when he switched from the *pro forma* delivery of "If you leave me – I'll go crazy! If you quit me – I'll go crazy! / If you forget me – I'll go crazy! Cause I love you, I love you, I love you – so much!" straight into the declaration that "You got to live / For yourself! / For yourself and nobody else!"

Or look at the fusion of sacred and profane in a best-selling contemporary artist directly descended from Brown: Prince Rogers Nelson. As with Sly Stone, George Clinton and go-go bandleader Chuck Brown, without Brown there would be no Prince. Even Nelson's earliest work – LPs like *For You* in 1978 and *Prince* in 1979 – features Jamesian funk basslines. But, during the 1980s, Princely innovation became dominant in pop. (*1999*'s commercial success was followed by the multimedia sweep of 1984's *Purple Rain*, '85's *Around The World In A Day*, *Parade*'s masterly "Kiss", '87's *Sign O The Times*, '88's *Lovesexy* and '89's *Batman*.) And a broad range of listeners had to realize that here, again, was a black American singer/composer/performer unwilling to separate sex and war, guilt and Armageddon, explicit physicality and old-time religion.

As critical periodical *Rock 'n' Roll Confidential* put it, "Little Richard pranced out the closet for all to see, James Brown *was* that sex machine, but on *Dirty Mind*, Prince really begins to talk about it, not just allude to it . . . he wants head; he wants her to get wet, he describes each thrust and parry . . . The sexual lyrics lead to liberation on a larger scale. By the end of *Dirty Mind*, Prince is singing 'You get out from under their power and you get some power of your own.' "

You can factor into Nelson's inheritance his own assimilation of those black vaudeville and comic theatre traditions James Brown had witnessed firsthand. And also the desire Prince demonstrates to recreate the spectacle of James Brown's Revue in his own stage shows. (Starting with the 1986 *Parade* tour and reaching an apotheosis with 1988's superb *Lovesexy* roadshow, Prince has shown he can even update Brown's *thang*: by harnessing female energies James had always suppressed. Drummer Sheila E, with her Latin/jazz base and female dancer Cat Glover – the perfect erotic foil for Prince – transformed the *Lovesexy* "tour" into funky world domination. And when Brown recorded his "Gimme Your Love" "duet" with Aretha Franklin – the two were in separate studios during Brown's final project before his jail term began – it was a radio remix by Prince which brought it real sexual pyrotechnics.)

Prince has a near-perfect grasp of the modern pop moment and how to manipulate it – the sort of savvy which, since 1975, no longer mediates Brown's own surrealist funk. Yet, during the early 1980s, a change in American demographics would bring James Brown to a whole new crowd: young, moneyed white folks.

Thanks to his 1978 *Animal House*, John Landis was Hollywood's highest-grossing director when he offered Brown a cameo in 1980's *The Blues Brothers*. The movie was conceived as a vehicle for comedians John Belushi and Dan Aykroyd – an extension of their *Saturday Night Live* television skits about a pair of white,

R'n'B-obsessed hipsters. Or, as John Landis described it: "a true musical which would use every great rhythm and blues performer we could get – an epic bizarre surreal picture of AMERICA with the Brothers as Christian Crusaders bringing back the blues!"

Landis maintains that all the black acts he featured – Aretha Franklin (who plays a waitress), Brown, Ray Charles and Cab Calloway – were thrilled to be in a movie and ecstatic to be associated with the celebrity of its white stars. ("James Brown? He couldn't wait to get on the plane. His only other movie was a thing called 'Ski Party A Go Go' [*sic*]"). Of all the African-Americans featured, Brown spent the least time filming his role as an acrobatic minister: a single day. And, according to John Landis, Brown was the only participant who did not suggest his tune be "done disco". (The director became confused by such crass contemporaneity among his black stars. But 70-year-old Cab Calloway, he says, attempted to explain: "The day we recorded 'Minnie the Moocher' was the 50th anniversary of the day Cab had written it – and he wanted to do it DISCO. I said, 'Cab, disco sucks' – it was written on all the cameras, 'Disco sucks'. I said, 'Cab, we want to bring back rhythm and blues.' He took me aside and said, 'John, I've done 'Minnie' Dixie and I've done it Charleston and I've done it rock and I've done it MOR.' He listed every fucking form of music for the last 50 years and he said, 'John – you do 'Minnie' for what the people want. You do music just for yourself and you're *jackin' off*.' ")

Brown says *he* had a different problem. "In 1978, you know, I went after the country and rock audience – I went after 'em big, through their clubs. And the *Blues Brothers* film was a help to me there."

"But," he continues, "I didn't know too much of what they

were about till I went and did the thing. You know, in it I play a
minister. But I didn't realize it was a comedy – so, there were
things I had to make 'em change. In order that I could play a
minister and not say anything wrong. When I found out it was
going to be a *comedy*, there were several changes I made."

The self-conscious, self-congratulatory style of *The Blues
Brothers* (for which the budget was $27 million as compared to
the $2.8 million of *Animal House*) helped define a new American
consumer who was emerging with the early '80s. This was the
yuppie, or young, upwardly-mobile (white) urban professional.
The yuppie market American merchandizers and ad firms would
soon be targeting invested the "classics" of soul (hits by Otis
Redding, James Brown, Sam and Dave) and the hits of Tamla-
Motown with a sentimental reverence they felt for anything
connected to their (white) youth. By the mid '80s, such music
was a constant in the fake '50s diners and singles clubs which had
sprung up around America. And cinemas were packed with a
nostalgic cameraderie – films like Barry Levinson's 1982 *Diner*
and Lawrence Kasdan's 1983 *The Big Chill*, which used vintage
Afro-American pop to articulate their "soul".

Near Brown's own birthplace in the Carolinas, a retro-musical
fad known as "beach music" sprang up. Critic John Morthland
described it as "an obsession for old novelty hits by black people
among kids to whom black people ARE a novelty". Everett
Caldwell, who designed a mid-'80s chain of '50s-style singles bars
and restaurants with names like "Studebaker's", realized such
yuppie nostalgia was *based* on fantasy. That the longings of this
new market ran no deeper than a desire to evoke the idea of
another age.

"Studebaker's is a trick," Caldwell told *Forth Worth Star*

Telegram reporter Casey Selix. "It's not anything like the (real) '50s. There are more remnants from the 1940s than the 1950s in Studebaker's: the Philip Morris signs, the Wurlitzer jukeboxes. The success of Studebaker's is what people *think* the '50s was." *The Blues Brothers* worked the same way. It was a film about the fact that yuppies – just like Landis, Belushi and Aykroyd – thought the '50s and '60s were "hip". And, when the film became a cult, that public's idea of hipnitude expanded to include James Brown.

For Brown, the yuppie dollar broke him free of disco tyranny on the airwaves. "Most acts need a hit to tour," says radio's Tom Joyner. "James never needed that. He may not have sold out the big halls during the '80s. But once he broke those white New Wave clubs, he could still tour all the time." And, because Brown had always set up his concerts as dance events, his act was perfect yuppie retro-entertainment. He offered expertise, familiar songs and a sense of ritual. His very elder-statesman status was an asset in itself.

"James had lost his radio," says white Southwestern promoter Angus Wynne III, who started booking Brown in the late '70s. "And the circuit he had worked was gone anyway. Back then, his band was looking kind of beat-up and terrified – it was not a luxury deal at all. James was having to hang on to every nickel."

But, says Wynne, who put the Godfather into clubs with names like Nick's Uptown, Fast and Cool, and The Lone Star Cafe, "James Brown could reach anyone who ever saw him onstage. Getting people *to* him was the only real problem."

During the past few years, Wynne maintains, Brown "could always get good money and was working out a regular circuit again. Plus, he always had anchor dates: big gigs for New Year's Eve, big society parties." In 1985, Wynne's brother, Shannon, had the outside wall of his Dallas club (named by both *Cosmopolitan* and *Playboy* as among yuppie America's "hottest") emblazoned with a gargantuan mural of James Brown in full scream.

Young, moneyed, Caucasian America had evolved an '80s religion of its own based on youth, leisure and financial gain. And the Hardest Working Man in Showbusiness emerged as one of its syncretic symbols – a process finalized when his 1985 contribution to Sylvester Stallone's *Rocky IV*, "Living In America", rocketed up the pop charts to No 5. Glossy and punchy, the song is relentlessly upbeat and upscale – a far cry from Brown's mid '70s discourses on Reality. But it brought JB a new contract. And, on his Dan Hartman-produced LP *Gravity* in 1986, it brought associations with stars from the white mainstream – figures as disparate as New Wave chanteuse Alison Moyet and '60s veteran Steve Winwood.

By even '83, however, Brown's *thang* had picked up. He cut the fiery "Bring It On, Bring It On" – a re-energized slice of mature funk – and put it out on his own regional independent. Maceo Parker and "chicken scratch" guitar ace Jimmy Nolen were back in his band. Nolen, who had joined Brown in 1965 and played with him over most of two decades, helped finalize the formula of funk. Yet his participation in Brown's comeback was brief: at the end of 1983, he suffered a fatal heart attack.

A series of re-issues was also helping to publicize the origins of Jamesian invention. America's Solid Smoke label released *Live at the Apollo* and two-parter *James Brown: The Federal Years* during 1983. And Briton Cliff White's long-delayed vinyl history of James began to trickle out – aided by a newly-sympathetic ear at Polydor in New York. (*Ain't That a Groove* and *Doin' It to Death*, excellent compilations by White featuring material from '66 to '73, were also released in the US in 1983.)

White had first approached Polydor as far back as 1976 – he wanted them to celebrate the 21st anniversary of "Please Please Please". They did so, with a *Solid Gold* double LP which is still in the catalogue. "That," says White, "was supposed to be the first of a whole series of double LPs chronicling James's career. But people kept leaving the company, so the second one – *Roots of a Revolution* – didn't come out until seven years later. It wasn't until a new guy, Tim Rogers, came into Polydor's US back catalogue office, that we started to get anywhere again. All the stuff which has come out since – like, in 1986, *In the Jungle Groove* and '88's *Motherlode* and the *James Brown's Funky People* series – has been done out of New York, with Tim."

Observers like Gerri Hirshey feel the yuppie-sparked renaissance of R'n'B smacked of the old, segregated fraternity-house gigs. "There was a lot going on in the early '80s – that's why I could sell my book. But the beach music and the *Blues Brothers* thing – although they offered work again to a lot of people who wanted it – was very like the original redneck circuit. Where frat-boys had soul acts play their affairs cause they wanted a total party mode. And only this real, serious music could provide it."

"It was very helpful to me," says Brown himself. "Not only did it bring me a brand new audience of young white folks. It also made people see me bein' truly diversified. In *The Blues Brothers*, they saw me able to deliver a message with gospel overtones. And, in the clubs, they saw a James Brown who went by people and not by colour. It wasn't the James Brown they thought they knew."

By 1987, Brown's latter statement was more than true: between November of that year and October '88, James and his third wife Adrienne managed to accumulate eight police arrests between them. Mrs Brown made repeated allegations of physical abuse by her spouse (including the claim that Brown fired shots into her Lincoln while she was inside it), but she declined to testify against him. At different times, both husband and wife were charged with possession of the proscribed drug phencyclidine – "PCP" or "angel dust", a veterinary tranquillizer. And, in October of '88, James spent four days in a Georgia hospital which specialized in treating drug abuse. (Adrienne Brown stayed almost a month at the same clinic.)

The events which preceded these had been equally traumatic. The man who once claimed that "hair and teeth" were the *sine qua non* of successful entertaining was treated for degenerative jaw disease with several rounds of excruciating surgery. During these ordeals, all Brown's real teeth were removed and his jaw was rebuilt so false teeth could be inserted. Shortly afterwards, on September 24, Brown interrupted an insurance seminar held in that Georgia "business park" where he maintains his offices (James Brown Enterprises and Top Notch Entertainment). Allegedly, he was waving a rifle. Then – in a recapitulation of the police chase three decades before (that time on foot) which landed his teenage self in prison – Brown led pursuing officers on a roundabout pursuit. By the time they managed to pull him over, the Godfather had crossed a state line. The following day, he was stopped again – only hours after making bail – for "driving under the influence".

In December of 1988, James Brown was convicted on two counts of aggravated assault and one count of failing to stop for police. His sentences: two six-year terms, set to run concurrently. Since the July 1989 discovery of the cash and cheques in his cell, some authorities say he has prejudiced any chance of an early parole. Others say he will be released by autumn of 1990 – or

August 1991. (Since April 12, 1990, he has been a part of the prison's "day release" work programme serving as a counsellor at the Aiken/Barnwell Counties Community Action Commission. Outside of working hours, he is confined to Aiken, South Carolina's minimum-security Lower Work Center facility.)

Although his parole dates have been set for March 1991 (South Carolina) and March 1992 (Georgia), no one can really predict the final outcome of Brown's incarceration. But from Jesse Jackson to rapper Melle Mel, numerous politicians and entertainment figures have campaigned for his early release. "They wouldn't have done it to Elvis or Frank Sinatra," says Afrika Bambaataa. "We just feel 'Look, if the man's got a problem – put him in a rehab scheme. Tell him, don't be comin' out here with guns.' Let that be part of the deal. To try and make an example of someone who helped this country so *much*, it's a sad comment on how we solve problems.

"Of course," he continues, "James gotta know in himself how things are with drugs and guns. Or, if you and your wife ain't gettin' along, well maybe it's time to jus' split up. But give this man a *break*."

History, at least, agrees with Bambaataa. Even as most of his old associates bemoan Brown's involvement with PCP – which they say he has nicknamed "the *go*-rilla" – they note that his music provides the very motor of hip-hop. And through this medium, James Brown continues to inspire: populating the world with would-be DJs and rappers, instilling in teens and pre-teens a hunger for the potency and power and humour of words.

"I just hate all the ways he's got himself tied up," says Bobby Byrd. "But, then again, it's never too late for change. Could be he's been doin' a lot of thinkin' in there."

saying it loud:
rap & '80s rarities

"You know, you can take a tape or a record to some very private spots: your room, your house, your car. And there you are with that music and your own private thoughts. Then next week there's the same performer that you had in the bedroom, performing live the same music you heard in those very inner places – in the dark, under the covers. There's just something about that, as opposed to computer stuff. That's where I think there is a magic about bein' who we are. The percentage of bein' that person – I don't know if it's greater or smaller or what percentage it is – but it's *there*. You know what I'm sayin'? That's what they callin' up when they tape-loop me or James."

Maceo Parker, 1989

"James Brown does what the hip-hop producer does with a high-tech, sophisticated, space-age machine. He samples with his throat and body. I don't fear any of these technocratic advances. Cause there will always be a James Brown to break it down, put it into the flesh, and play it back."

Robert Farris Thompson, 1989

For many critics, it is James Brown's articulation of soul which marks him as a colossus among American artists. Yet, among those peoples of the diaspora best qualified to judge, his primary legacy is the funk sensibility: a complex fabric of attitudes, rhythms, sentiments and spiritual poise which circulates recurring concerns about human expressiveness and potential.

Inherent in this sensibility – and central to Brown's importance – is the demonstration that language alone cannot do justice to the dispersal and flow of black cultures and philosophies over the past two centuries. That words, unaided, cannot embrace the density and play of allusions in which black expressive practices rejoice. For, as Dr Paul Gilroy has noted, these practices disseminate remarkably subversive power – a power to change "what counts as history and reality . . . what names mean, what *reference* means". With his fine fine superfine funk, James Brown constructed a *de facto* black liberation theology.

Brown's personal genius is thrown into sharpest relief by movement; movement away from one thing and towards another. For him, idealism and striving take the form of dancing, of getting on the good foot and feeling the funk. It should come as no surprise that the singer feels most comfortable, most liberated in motion. After all, his life has been shaped by the pull of opposing forces: utter need and total denial, identity and invisibility, isolation and adulation, freedom and life behind bars. James Brown willed himself to create out of tension, and tensions – sexual, moral, ethical – now define his funk. "Why such unrest? Why so strident?" Joyce Carol Oates once asked about the boxers Brown idolizes and imitates in his orbit of perpetually defensive motion. The answer she came up with: because "this world is conceived in anger – and in hatred, and in hunger – no less than it is conceived in love."

Home, as Gerri Hirshey says in *Nowhere to Run*, "is a tricky concept if you've been told to move along for a century and a half." But black cultures learn to recreate a psychological, spiritual dwelling-place from moment to moment, via the living event. Worship, carnal passion, performance – all are centrally linked in this drive for immediate meaning and continual transcendence. "The live event, yes Ma'am!" says James Brown, with lipsmacking gusto. "Your mainstream entertainer today is evading that element. If you don't want to involve yourself, if you can't learn to extend yourself, how deep is the impression you make? Where do you stand with history?"

Even as he lounges in a "correctional facility" speculating into a telephone, Brown's *thang* is abroad in the world, spreading the restless, probing urges of its creator. James Brown records have affected Caribbean reggae, the pan-Afro pop of the black Mother Continent, the hip-hop of New York's Bronx. "A tune like Brown's 'Say It Loud, I'm Black and I'm Proud' or 'I Don't Want Nobody to Give Me Nothin', Open Up the Door and I'll Get It Myself'," says Jamaican-born poet and music historian Linton Kwesi Johnson, "had a deep effect on my thinking and my development, on my own soul. It was my introduction to American singers, black artists, talking about things which were relevant and meaningful – a whole cultural movement hand-in-hand with the political movement of Black Power."

In the evolution of popular sound, Caribbean black musics have played a central role – a fact which European critics have been very slow in acknowledging. That same New Orleans which gave James Brown what Robert Farris Thompson calls his "high-octane fusion of African musics" has long been regarded as more Caribbean than American. And, through its '50s R'n'B – the work of artists like Fats Domino, as well as Jamesian favourites like Roy Brown – New Orleans helped to nourish the roots of Jamaican reggae. Linton Kwesi Johnson: "During the Second World War, the Yankees had a base in Jamaica at Vernon Fields, and there the black soldiers were segregated from the whites. The whites would bring down their Tin Pan Alley-type music and the blacks their be-bop and their R'n'B.

"Jamaicans developed a taste for all this. And the way reggae evolved was first of all when they couldn't get the R'n'B any more, the sound system operators started hiring the locals to do R'n'B tunes. But, after a while, our own folk and religious forms took over. So that the only thing left in the music from that jazz and blues influence was this offbeat emphasis, this thing about the off beat." The legacy, in fact, of that same "New Orleans beat" Pee Wee Ellis recalls as central to the genesis of Jamesian funk.

The Caribbean "sound" or sound system, with its huge amplifiers, its emphasis on the heaviness of the "bottom" or bassline, and its flamboyant, talkative DJs and MCs (including "toasters" who rapped over instrumental sides) was exported wherever West Indians migrated. From the mid '70s on, this fact would alter American culture – and, in the process, bring James Brown to yet another generation.

That process began in '73, with the emergence in New York's South Bronx (a poor borough bruised by violent warfare between youth gangs) of a DJ called Kool Herc. Herc had come to New York from Kingston only six years before, and his turntable style was taken from Jamaica's toasting DJs. He adapted it with disco records – rather than the heavy dub plates in use back home. And, as *Village Voice* critic Steven Hager wrote in 1982, "Herc was the first DJ to buy records just for a 15-second instrumental solo, which he would play over and over, while at the same time talking over a microphone connected to an echo chamber... a kind of primitive rapping, consisting mainly of new slang words and an occasional joke which might be making the rounds at local high schools . . .Talking on the microphone during a party became a favourite pastime and everyone wanted to get in on the act."

What an understatement! Herc's now-legendary parties, with voices rapping to specially-chosen instrumental "breaks", helped spawn an entire new school of acrobatic movement – "break dancing". Young bloods whose aggressive energies and lust for identity might have led them to street gangs turned instead to competitive feats like "headspins" and "finger rolls", evolving entire genres like the "electric boogie" and "body-popping". Its practitioners, soon known as "b-boys", showed a preference for athletic gear, baseball caps and Pro-Ked tennis shoes. Many of those original b-boys would follow in Herc's grooves directly, by later becoming DJs themselves.

In 1975, a Black Muslim with a fetish for vinyl obscurities graduated from a South Bronx high school called Stevenson – and was rewarded by his Barbadian mom with a set of DJ turntables. Afrika Bambaataa (a name which means "affectionate leader") had once been a violent, coldblooded ganglord. But, after viewing Cy Enfield's '63 movie epic *Zulu*, Bambaataa decided to found a new sort of "social club": one he dubbed the Zulu Nation. Born again with a b-boy social conscience, Bam devoted his Zulus "to funk". And, by November of 1976, he was making his mark as a serious DJ. In sound system battles which recalled the intense rivalries (and colourful bad-boy tactics) of the Caribbean, Bam and his Zulu nationals would face off the troops of Kool Herc.

Through them, and around them, a new musical art was evolving. It started with Herc's rapping; then expanded through Bam's notoriously eclectic taste in sounds. Hager: "During one legendary battle with Disco King Mario, Bambaataa opened his show with the theme song from *The Andy Griffith Show*, taped off his television set. He mixed the ditty with a rocking drum beat, followed it with *The Munsters* theme song and quickly changed gears with 'I Got The Feeling' by James Brown." Within a single year, these club and sound system spectacles were transformed again, by another West Indian – Joseph Sadler, also known as "Grandmaster Flash" – and a DJ known locally by the moniker Grand Wizard Theodor.

In 1985's *Fresh*, critic Nelson George defined Sadler's contribution as a complete change: "Flash's concept was to turn the turntable on itself, making it a musical instrument in its own right. He did this by rubbing the needle against the groove, instead of allowing the needle to play the record normally ... The result was Jimi Hendrix's alien sound with a basic James Brown beat. Flash took this noise and would either make it the beat or make it play against the beat of a second record he was playing."

The art of manipulating a record back and forth with the needle still in its groove for percussive emphasis ("scratching") had been happened upon by DJ Theodor, while listening to himself backspin in order to "cue up" a play. And, added to the mixing miracles these street DJs were perpetrating, scratching put the creation of new sound from old within anyone's reach. Flash,

Bam, Herc and Theodor created turntable art; they used repetition, juxtaposition, noise and rhythm like sorcerers.

And they had plenty of apprentices. From '77 to '79, the Bronx bubbled like an underground research lab, with breakdancers, rappers, mixers and DJs (not to mention their visual sidekicks, the graffiti squads or "taggers" and "bombers") expanding the original styles almost daily. People began to refer to these new, connected genres as "hip-hop". And hip-hop became less tangential when, in 1979, two rap records – The Fatback Band's "Tim III (Personality Jock)" and The Sugarhill Gang's "Rapper's Delight" – were pressed and released. The first was a commercial failure. The second shipped 2 million copies, founded an independent label, and initiated a musical revolution. Come the '80s, that *coup* would preserve vinyl from the tyranny of the compact disc, and it would redistribute power and influence within much of the music establishment. Hip-hop, in fact, would make good on the empty promises of punk. Because of Herc, Flash, Bam, Theodor and those who followed, as Paul Gilroy puts it, "the everyday technology of consumption has been redefined to become an instrument with which music can be produced."

Rapidly, the new DJs also discovered sequencers and digital sampling – electronic modes of thievery by means of which any existing sound could be fixed within a computer's brain, looped and then called up to be played back in any key and tempo. Sampling made the cutting, mixing and scratching of live clubs into a studio art and gave the curiosity of music creators from Afrika Bambaataa to Branford Marsalis unlimited scope. By 1989, critics were talking about a "new Harlem renaissance – on floppy disk" (Barry Michael Cooper, *Village Voice*); as the '90s began, *The New York Times*' Jon Pareles termed hip-hop "both the most startlingly original and the fastest-growing genre in popular music". Yet the epicentre of all this action is still commanded by a single figure: James J Brown, the FOREFUNKFATHER of it all.

In manifold ways, hip-hop is his child. No 1, Brown's beats provide much of the whole art's foundation. Before sampling made it possible to repossess Maceo's soulful squeal, Jabo's different strokes or JB's personal shrieks, when the whole hip-hop experience was still live on club turntables or hot-wired out of lamps in the parks and streets (early, free electric sources) b-boys would scour New York in search of old Brown 45s. Stuck onto larger vinyl – for better mixing grip – these copies of "Sex Machine", "Funky Drummer" or "Get Up, Get Into It and Get Involved" would be mixed with sounds as diverse as The Incredible Bongo Band's version of "Apache" or Grand Central Station's "The Jam".

The initial aural battles in the Bronx, with their gangs of flamboyant breakers and fiercely loyal, competitive troops, may seem light years away from the ritualized theatrics of the James Brown Revue. But a DJ working his "tables" and his club crowd together as one recreates the very sort of excitement Mr Dynamite sought to ignite. This, too, is a *thang* which draws on funk, musical memory, sound history and sophisticated expressive skills. (Mixing and scratching require a fiendish degree of musical knowledge and eye-to-hand dexterity; few who have only watched it can fully appreciate the task.)

From the very first, hip-hop's public paid tribute to James Brown – every year, Bam's Zulu Nation would hold a special evening of homage. Then, in 1982, with help from records by Kraftwerk, Ennio Morricone, and Captain Sky, producers Tom Silverman – owner of Tommy Boy – and Arthur Baker, his rappers

Soul Sonic Force and a Roland TR808 drum machine, Afrika Bambaataa created a record called "Planet Rock". A club and marketing hit, it shipped gold shortly after release. "Planet Rock" made Bam a STAR – and, from the platform it gave him, he started to praise James Brown in the press.

The points Bam reiterated were basic to hip-hop as a regenerative black art. With only the marketplace for a context, he noted, funk would never gain recognition for its true importance. Commercial sales could never provide any real indication of the links that funk had forged, the tales it had to tell, the complex of allusions it embodied. But hip-hop, as Bambaataa stressed, could put these things in their proper perspective. Hip-hop could give Brown's funk a *black* context, an historical and spiritual connectedness.

After all, he says, "James helped to *show* us we was black – not 'Negro'! *Teach* us how we was black. Then people wanted to get away from blackness. Today they still arguing over whether this is Negro colour, black American, African-American – all that stuff. Well, before anything else, you was BLACK. And what James Brown taught us is: you just gotta deal with that fact."

"James was a primary influence on the lives of all DJs and rappers. For bringin' that funk, and for the dancin' and for the excitement he caused on the crowd. His funk expresses what the Zulu Nation is really about. There is power in James Brown's music: the *down* bass, the groove, the TALK. He talked that talk. He had so many sayin's, from them came a whole new vocabulary. It still has people writin' up big books about *black* English."

Academic Farris Thompson agrees with Bam. "Hip-hop makes even the phrase 'this here person' seem quite chic. There's so much power in this music it can make even the arbiters of language have to shut up. Hip-hop crystallizes around James Brown not least because he's so *playful.* He's so self-conscious about his blackness – his whole funk theology, his funky empire, his funk ambiance."

"Most definitely he also changed how people hear music," says Bambaataa. "For instance, he's the first one really made what you call a 'disco' record – long-playin' records, 'Part 1', 'Part 2', 'Volume 3'. Sixteen-minute 'Sex Machine', stuff like that. The same groove and the same bass line goin' on and on. Adding grunts and moans and sometimes sayin' something – and sometimes sayin' nothin', you know?" Bam grins. "Just like on his record: 'Talkin' Loud and Sayin' Nothing'."

In Britain, the teen hip-hop scene sparked by Bambaataa's own loud-talking funk would become massive – and it was fully multi-cultural. "For us as Britons," says Max L-X, a DJ who, with his partner Dave V-J, rose to prominence on the illegal "pirate" radio airwaves, "hip-hop was the first music that could seriously say it had a multi-racial element. It didn't belong to any one group – and no particular race could say 'it's ours'." James Brown was always a symbolic part of that cultural mix. White hip-hop DJ Tim Westwood (one of the first pirate spinners to make it onto a primetime, commercial London station): "We were playing Brown for the dancers, the breakers and bodypoppers – from the very earliest, streetstyle British jams. Stuff like 'Get On The Good Foot'; breakdancing used to be called 'goodfoot', after that record."

In 1984, Bambaataa himself decided to rap with his mentor and inspiration. The result was that year's "Unity (Peace, Love and Havin' Fun)" – a six-part rap duet with Brown, with a matching video. "We went back to some of his old grooves to make it comfortable for him," says Bam. "But, of course, all the time he'd be tellin' me, 'I been that!', 'I did that before!' He likes the rappers, though. He says Michael Jackson and Prince and myself are like his children."

In ten years, rap and sampling have changed the entertainment mainstream completely. Although rappers from LL Cool J to Young MC have sold millions without airplay, trade Bible *Billboard* now prints a "Rap Singles" Chart as well as its "Top Black Singles" and "Hot Dance Music" charts. And that old boundary between "black" and "white" musics – "soul" and "pop" – has been stretched to near breaking point. After all, artists as established as Quincy Jones, Prince, Janet Jackson and Madonna are now scrambling to sample (not to mention more commercial institutions such as McDonalds and Burger King).

Then there is the USA's *Arsenio Hall Show*. Every weeknight, on primetime US TV, a 33-year-old African-American named Arsenio Hall holds court on America's No 1-ranked national chat show. (With the under-35 audience, Hall ranked No 1 even before he broke Johnny Carson's two-decade lock on the top slot.) As frequently dressed in hip-hop sports gear as he is in streamlined designer suits, Hall is using TV to introduce whites to black America. Some critics argue that the network star's merchandising of black street style is a calculated business move. Certainly, its impact parallels Brown's bombshell appearances of twenty years before. And on May 3, 1989, Hall leans into the camera and makes a birthday speech to James Brown. "I want to say thank you, James," he concludes, "because without *you*, I would never be here."

Watching such post hip-hop tributes from prison, it's hard to imagine how Brown must feel. At times, he has been bitter about the fact that, as veteran rapper Melle Mel (lead voice in

Grandmaster Flash's original Furious Five) told *Rolling Stone*: "Everybody samples James Brown. You can't make a rap record without sampling some James Brown." (Mel's claim is borne out by even a cursory listen to hits from, among others, Run-DMC, Eric B & Rakim, the Beastie Boys, Double D and Steinski, Ice-T, Big Daddy Kane, Roxanne Shant, Sweet Tee, Spoonie Gee, EPMD, DJ Mark the 45 King, Kool Moe Dee, Schoolly D, The Classical Two, Kid 'n' Play, SuperLover Cee and Casanova Rud, the D.O.C., Rob Base and DJ EZ Rock, the Stone Roses, Fine Young Cannibals, or Public Enemy.) In 1988, Brown turned a rap with admirers Full Force ("I'm Real") into a very specific protest. "All of you people / think you got pull," he growled, "Better get your names off my records / till I'm PAID IN FULL."

At dinner with old friend Cliff White after accepting a special award at Britain's March 1988 DMC (Disco Mix Club) Championships, Brown betrayed confusion about a reception so rapturous White himself had been stunned. "It was quite amazing standing with him behind that curtain in the Royal Albert Hall, and seeing the place just packed with street kids! It was such a charged atmosphere. Then, when they announced 'James Brown' – which had been a well-kept secret – and pulled back the drapes, it was just like the Beatles. Pandemonium!

"But back at the hotel," says White, "every once in a while, James would go back to the evening and say, 'But why didn't they ask me to sing? What was I really there for? Why wasn't I asked to sing a song?' He really didn't seem to know what it *meant*."

Eighteen months later, however, Brown has grown accustomed to his place as hip-hop's founder. "Ninety per cent of the rap songs," he says with pride, "have my music in those grooves. It's a very great compliment to me." After a slight pause he adds, "So I guess I oughta *accept* it."

In common with other sampled artists, Brown has little real choice. Now that hip-hop has brought in big bucks, there have been a series of lawsuits over the possible copyright infringements of ancient beats. But the onetime DJs of hip-hop have also become a new breed of record producer (what American critic Greg Tate calls a "consortium of beat-boppers, mega-mix researchers, sound collage technicians"). And most are well-armed with legal muscle. Many samples destined for the charts now appear by virtue of already agreed-upon fees. Otherwise, they can still be legally defended, on grounds of "fair use" ("creative, parodic or scholarly appropriation").

Ken Anderson, a lawyer for several rap acts (including the Beastie Boys, who settled out of court over their theft of a saxophone hit from '70s disco group Wild Sugar), stressed the new form's density to *Village Voice* critic Charles Aaron. Most listeners, says Anderson, make the assumption hip-hop art is "completely linear and (that), at any one moment, only one sample is occurring ... But we're talking ... about depths of layers of sound." Listening, in other words, to the polyphonic, poly-semic, polyrhythmic universe of James Brown: the point in time where slang, soul, showbiz and humour conspire together to highlight their roots.

Rap itself has become too vast, too regional, too quicksilver and responsive to generalize about. There is now high-art rap (like Quincy Jones's star-studded, "educational" LP *Back On The Block*), unrepentantly streetwise rap (like Schoolly D's *Am I Black Enough For You?*, which shamelessly lifts track titles themselves like "Mama Feelgood" or "Get Off Your Ass and Get Involved" from James Brown's repertoire), rap which carries on 200-year-old traditions of African-American vaudeville (like De La Soul or

Jazzy Jeff and the Fresh Prince), novelty raps (like Tone-Loc's "Wild Thing", which surpassed all sales of single records, except those of "We Are The World"), bedroom raps, knowledge raps, "raga-rap" influenced by reggae rhythms and Caribbean *patois*, revenge raps, message raps, anti-apartheid raps, black power raps, hippie raps – even the "fat boy" raps popularized by groups like Heavy D and The Boys, The Fat Boys and Arsenio Hall's alter ego, "Chunky A". There is a burgeoning army of female rappers. And, already, there are the genre's "classic voices" – originals like Kurtis Blow, Melle Mel, Kool Moe Dee and Run-DMC – followed by distinctive "New Jacks" like LL Cool J, Big Daddy Kane and MC Hammer. There are old posses and new pretenders – and, by the time you read this, there will be plenty more.

And above them all, when it comes to Jamesian influence, there are Public Enemy and NWA (Niggers With Attitude). From direct steals – saxophones, guitar riffs, screams, spoken phrases and similar breaks – through direct allusions ("another summer / sound of the Funky Drummer"), all rappers stand in James Brown's shadow. But, in completely different ways, these two crews have carried on where he left off.

Public Enemy take their name from a 1972 Brown track, "Public Enemy No 1". And they make the densest, growlingest, most direct Black Advancement hip-hop imaginable; a sound which comes across as the compleat urban machine. Their trade-off between vocal timbres (messenger Chuck D is billed as "the bass", comedian Flavor Flav as "the treble") and their marriage of depth to rhythm recalls Brown and his JBs at their hottest, "workin' out". And, although it has been denied extensive radio airplay, Public Enemy's music has been more widely dispersed thanks to independent African-American film-maker Spike Lee. Their "Fight The Power" is used to articulate the basic themes of his 1989 American masterpiece *Do the Right Thing*.

By the end of the 1980s, the fortunes of young black America had suffered a serious decline. Below the age of eighteen, almost half the black population was living in poverty. Particularly among males, African-American college enrollment had fallen dramatically and more young black men were incarcerated than at any other point in US penal history. (A Washington DC-based advocacy group, The Sentencing Project, claims in its 1989 report that up to 23 percent of young African-American males between the ages of twenty and twenty-nine are under some kind of penal supervision.) A National Research Council report issued in July of 1989 states that "the status of blacks relative to whites has stagnated or regressed since the early 1970s". A five-year report from The University of Chicago's Population Research Center published the following month concludes that segregation has "deepened" in 10 out of the 60 major US cities studied – and that segregation in all 60 is "worse than had been imagined". As if this were not enough, the late '80s crack industry holds many poor black American communities – particularly the inner-city young – in a virtual state of siege.

Unlike other teen musics, rap reflects all these changes. Like the black preacher, it chooses a vocabulary and reference points familiar to the least-enfranchised listener. And, like the great soul poets, it teaches that transcendence can be found right on the street: through rhythm, invention and energy. Rap relates creative black history – proud, just as Spike Lee is proud, to deal in the language of the "underclass".

Public Enemy share their Godfather's concern for education.

"By now I wonder how / Some people never know / The enemy could be their friend, guardian / I'm not a hooligan / I rock the party and / Clear all the madness, I'm not a racist / Preach to teach all," Chuck D declares in "Don't Believe The Hype". A 5-minute, 20-second degree in Contemporary Urban Studies, "Don't Believe The Hype" urges black youth to think for themselves – to form their own opinions, both about rap and the world at large. In this respect, it typifies all of Public Enemy's work, which resonates with pride in those arts which compose hip-hop. ("This jam may hit or miss the charts / But the style gets wild / As state of the art.")

Public Enemy are "militant" about most things. Founder-member Professor Griff's espousal of the Nation of Islam head, Louis Farrakhan (whose recklessness with rhetoric Griff shares), almost caused the group to collapse from media pressure on several occasions during 1989 and early 1990. The crew's logo is the silhouette of a "homeboy" caught in the cross-hairs of a rifle sight. And, at shows, their onstage guard – "The Security of the First World" – point models of Uzi machine guns at the audience.

Public Enemy have endowed academic scholarships for ghetto students to attend black universities. They perform in schools and prisons as well as on the concert stage. But does their programme for change come at the expense of Jews, whites or gays? In light of quotes from Professor Griff and debatable interpretations of Public Enemy's 1990 "Welcome To the Terrordome" single, some critics have argued yes. But at the inception of this controversy (much of it obviously conducted with one eye on circulation figures), as white critic Robert Christgau pointed out, "there's no discernible homophobia or anti-Semitism – and only a touch of reverse racism – in the crew's recorded work". Some of Professor Griff's behaviour has certainly seemed questionable.

Yet his remarks can do little to negate his group's accomplishments. And, like Minister Farrakhan (whose words, contentious as they are, have also often been deliberately misrepresented by the media), Professor Griff stepped over an old line ... the one which says a black man must always be more careful than his Caucasian counterparts. That, as Amiri Baraka noted twenty-seven years ago, black Americans must always be seen to *deserve* their equality. The idea that this could still be the case when you are offered no education, no job, no role in the real American scenario – this is what Public Enemy (just like James Brown) are about.

Niggers With Attitude – five friends from the rough Los Angeles suburb of Compton – have carried a different facet of the James Brown legacy into rap. Their province is stylizing, and then selling, what they have. In NWA's case, this means the world of the gang-riddled Compton streets, with their predatory police force, their drug-dominated lifestyle, their adolescent machismo. Because the group's founder Eazy-E (aka Eric Wright) is a unique rapper and their Dr Dre a "dope" (state-of-the-art) producer, this hardcore vision makes perfect teen-rap fodder.

It's also great late '80s *lit noir*, though main writer Ice Cube – who in early 1990 left the group to work with Public Enemy's producers – prefers the term "journalism". NWA singles are sharp, if often obscene: "Dopeman" (a sardonic portrait of a pusher), "Boyz 'n the 'Hood" (a sardonic portrait of the young lives around them) and "Radio" (a comic-sardonic comment about the "democracy" of the airwaves). They've even produced a hip-hop anthem to self-expression – an anti-drug rap with lines like, "Blame it on Ice Cube / Because he said it / Gets funky when you got / A subject and a predicate," ("Express Yourself"). And all their best tunes embody to the Nth degree that basic pop requirement of *catchiness.*

Although, in another age, they've done exactly what he did, James Brown – like many older blacks – might feel NWA "discredit" their own community. But in celebrating that all the young black underclass has to call its own – its youth and its blackness – NWA offers genuine updates of Brown originals like "Say It Loud" and "I Don't Want Nobody To Give Me Nothing". Undeniably, their message is getting across to African-American youth – as well as some of their white counterparts. And this has forced cultural commentators, even educators, to concede the power and depth of that communication. The January 1990 issue of *Jet* magazine carries a report of a two-day symposium at Glassboro State College in New Jersey, at which speaker Dr Houston Baker (Director of the University of Pennsylvania's Center for the Study of Black Literature and Culture) maintained that anyone who couldn't relate to rap was "not fit to teach".

"There is every reason," said Baker, "for believing you can teach Public Enemy or NWA in the context of that play *Antigone*. It's about the individual versus the authority, the state. And so much of what's going on in the black inner city these days has to do with the feeling that the state, in the person of the police, as NWA put it, is trying to suppress or repress individual rights."

One must add to the NWA saga Eric Wright's acumen as an entrepreneur. Wright is the sole owner of Ruthless Records, a hip-hop independent distributed through Warners, Atlantic and Priority (the compilation label run by a former K-Tel supremo). By 1989, Ruthless product included: six Dre-helmed rap LPs, three gold and headed for platinum sales; the "uncensored" NWA video-album, and the Dre-produced debut of a Dallas, Texas rapper who calls himself The D.O.C. – sold to Atlantic Records for one million dollars. For that year, each member in NWA took home a six-figure salary, and the D.O.C. produced one of 1990's first No 1 rap singles. As short and spiky as Mr Dynamite himself, Eazy Eric Wright is also exactly the same sort of prescient music-biz professional. "He's the most Machiavellian guy I've ever met," Wright's manager (30-year white music biz veteran Jerry Heller) told *LA Weekly* journalist Jonathan Gold. "He instinctively knows about power and how to control people. And his musical instincts are infallible."

In 1975, while hip-hop was being invented in the Bronx, a separate Jamesian renaissance was brewing 4,000 miles away in the capital of Great Britain. It, too, began with DJs – first-generation black Britons whose ears were schooled by the reggae "sounds", and white collector-fanatics who ran clothes shops and one-nighter clubs. Together, during the early '80s, they would combine a mushrooming club scene with the power of "pirate" radio, to create a massive funk fad which would come to be known as "rare groove". The gods of this '85–'86 phenomenon (which paralleled the UK rise of hip-hop and brought about a new unity among young Londoners of all races) were Brown and his JBs.

The term "rare groove" was coined by Norman Joseph, aka Norman Jay. Now a member of Phonogram Records' A & R team, Jay was then a pirate jock on London's "unlicensed" broadcaster KISS-FM. At the moment Bambaataa and Herc were recharging the Bronx, says Joseph, things were very different across the water. "In '75–'76, it was unheard of for British black kids to be into R'n'B. R'n'B was, in this country, part of the white way of life. That whole scene here was run by white people. People with that English conservative-eccentric attitude, that when you're into something deeply you treasure it, collect it and you're very protective about it. The stereotypes were set, you know – if you're black, you're into reggae; if you're white, you can be into what you want." Jay was "the only kid in my school who was into R'n'B". (Norman's dreadlocked brother Joey, by contrast, was and is the head of Good Times, one of London's best-known reggae "sounds".)

Between '67 and '77, James Brown only made the British pop charts once (in 1976, with "Get Up Offa That Thing" at No 22). But all during the '70s, his records remained staple plays at London clubs such as Hunters and Countdown – leisure haunts patronized by an older, black clientele. Then in the early '80s, at "warehouse parties" (illegal, pay-at-the-door affairs) and West End niteries such as Gullivers, the Casses Club, the Beat Route and the Wag, funk fanatics Barrie Sharpe, Lascelles Gordon, Femi Williams, Marco Nelson, Steve Lewis, Paul "Trouble" Anderson and Jonathon More began to command the turntables. By 1985, Sharpe, Gordon and Anderson were running a weekly club of their own – The Cat In The Hat, located in "downtown" London's Leicester Square. And during that same year, a young white DJ and all-round hustler, Gordon MacNamee, launched a pirate station called KISS-FM. "Gordon Mac" recruited the city's best club DJs – and he gave Norman Jay the show which would really create "rare groove".

Rare groove was re-exhumed '70s funk (the more obscure the better), especially anything by James Brown or his various band members. But rare groove was more than just music; rare groove the *phenomenon* was a different sort of *thang*. It was a public culmination of massive changes in the UK's capital: the rebirth of record shops as real teenage hangouts; the public debut of a new youth dance culture; and an explosion of radio pirates playing those musics – black musics – Londoners had been denied by legal broadcasting and established record companies. For Norman Jay, the funk came alive *because* this moment mattered. And, once again, James Brown was telling it like it had to be told: "It was *live* again, you see. With warehouse parties and one-off clubs, we created the right environment for it to work. Playing those records that time around, I was hearing them in a way I had never done before." When Jay launched his "Rare Groove Show" on KISS-FM, he says, "the one thing I felt above all was that, as a black man, it was my moral duty to get behind this music, to tell its story. So that's what I did."

Jay meant a bigger story than just the history of James Brown and his JBs, the music they constructed and the way that music changed. He meant the whole panoply of a diaspora and its peoples – connected by an underground of musical reference points. Norman's funk is a folk history in itself: "I feel very strongly about that; no matter in what form music evolves, it's always relative to its history. Some people know the literal history, even which guy opened the door to the toilet in the studio. But I've got no interest in that, that's of no importance to me. What's important is what it *did*; what the music helps me relate to, how it affected a given time in my life. I used to say that on KISS – that most of these records, for somebody, somewhere, were unlocking a painful or a beautiful memory."

Almost overnight, the rare groove cult exploded into a major fad. On London's thirty pirate stations, funk obscurities soon dominated the playlist – spinning side-by-side with the latest hip-hop imports. Record fairs became the scene of cut-throat competition, with Jamesian rarities like *Hell* or *Damn Right I Am Somebody* changing hands for up to £50 ($90) apiece. And, for young black DJs, hustling the actual vinyl – *after* they had publicized it over the pirate waves – offered a form of alternative employment. So did the manufacture of bootleg rarities, or "booties", which were soon flooding the specialist record shops.

Rare groove turned London's commercial radio network, with its rigid formats and ossified playlisting, upside-down. Mainstream white DJs became desperate for the hottest plays – and found themselves combing secondhand stalls, at the mercy of young black Britons who knew funk music's history by heart. "The real truth of 'rare groove'," said KISS-FM DJ Trevor "Madhatter" Nelson at the end of '87, "lies in the hustling of music and the exploitation of another man's knowledge. There's no real money to be made in DJing on this scene; it's not like commercial radio, where your phone rings every minute. The money comes from moving the vinyl."

The real entrepreneurs of rare groove were black Londoners like Trevor. Kids who worked in record shops or for wholesalers, and DJ'd on the side. Kids who quickly turned their knowledge into an income for themselves. "In 1985, we started getting stuff and *making* it big," says Nelson. "We'd even do it with rubbish. We'd just say, 'this is good, mate – I want 20 quid.' And we'd get it." Major labels like Polydor were soon scrambling to recruit these underground DJs, because they needed to be told what saleable rare grooves lay in their own back catalogues.

By 1988, the British capital was swamped with '70s style – trendies had adopted Afro wigs, platform soles, floppy hats and "roadblock" flares. The Cat in The Hat spawned its own shop, Barrie Sharpe's The Duffer of St George. And no less than three sets of black pirate DJs were involved in setting up new, independent record stores: the Soul II Soul shop in North London, West London's Vinyl Lab (which would, as Black Market

Records, later establish its team in the central West End) and Soho's Red Records. In 1989, even the government would concede things had changed, and award KISS-FM a licence to broadcast legally. Today, the hustlers of UK rare groove are respectable, if unorthodox, businessmen – the owners of cars, houses, radio shares and portable phones.

But before that, back in the spring of 1988, those men who had made rare groove decided to try something unprecedented: they wanted to stage a reunion of the whole James Brown Revue. The project began at a meeting of two London crews ("Family Funktion" and "Shake & Finger Pop") who had often combined to throw regular "raves" or one-off parties.

"We were all round in my bedroom one night," says Norman Jay. "We had booked this date at the Town and Country Club, and we had to come up with some sort of live act. 'I Know You Got Soul' was spinning on my turntable and I just turned to Femi and Marco and said 'Imagine Bobby Byrd at the Town & Country with us – man, that would be so wicked!' The next night I went down the Wag Club. And Marco walked up to me and said, 'Guess what – I phoned Bobby Byrd, and he's coming.' I was absolutely staggered."

"Me and my wife was lyin' in bed in Springfield, Tennessee," says Bobby Byrd, "when this kid from London phones up and starts tellin' me how big our tunes are over there. After he hung up, me and Vicki just looked at each other and laughed. We just thought, 'someone's *jokin*'!'. We were used to oldies stations and so on. But we never heard of no pirates."

On the strength of counsel from Charles Bobbitt and Cliff White (as well as a round-trip ticket), Bobby and Vicki made the journey, played the Town and Country – and came home thoroughly flabbergasted. "I could not *believe* it!" says Byrd today. "There was people knew the first record I ever recorded, the first tunes James ever sung, everything Vicki had done. When we got out to the club Vicki said, 'Just *look* at this crowd, Bobby. Let's just go outside and see if they've got James Brown's name on the marquee.' "

Anderson was stunned – after over twenty years, Brown's associates were enjoying the kind of solo stardom they'd only dreamt of. On July 20 and 21, 1988, almost the whole crew of JBs was re-united on the Town and Country stage. The gigs were so packed and emotionally charged, so *crowded* that those who attended could hardly open the toilet doors. And individual numbers, like "Across The Tracks" or "Pass The Peas", were greeted with ovations which would have deafened a football stadium.

"Some people could hardly speak," says Norman Jay. "I mean, we didn't know what these people *looked like.* All we had to go on was the old, old records and photographs. Then, here they were – here they all WERE! And the only one missing was James. Which somehow even seemed fitting."

Especially to some of these women Brown had so often shunted aside. "Martha High," says Anderson, "was with James twenty years, yet she never had one real solo performance until that night. Of course, we'd all had *spots.* But like me, like Lyn and Marva, you had to sing just what James Brown wanted, even down to the key. You were always screamin' your lungs out, or bassin' – just so you could be HEARD."

Five years after those memorable nights, "rare groove" has passed into UK social history. Hip-hop is less a spontaneous live event than a massive, world-wide commodity. Yet, at the same moment, James Brown himself is back in detention every night.

Yet the permutations of culture he made possible have engineered awakenings Brown could never have foreseen. His voice is now a key on the sampling machines of the world – the telegraph of new generations. The musicians he drew together twenty years ago constitute a living pantheon, a human alphabet of funk. And his work can now be recognized for the spiritual conjugation it is.

For the Jamesian funk is more crucible than gut-bucket: it factors tradition into vision, then translates vision into belief. Hip-hop has brought its discourse into an electronic age, a world barraged by fragments and pieces and imagery lacking context. Yet, even within this atomized arena, funk's African principle triumphs – shaping hip-hop art through montage, through repetition, through faith in the essential relationship of all things. Real meaning, it tries to teach us, emerges from real, human connectedness. That deep bond reaches far beyond words. Yet it is the *thang* James Brown has always been talking about.

ain't that a groove!

"I've lived in my country – Britain – my whole life. And I think to myself, how many black people now own a club? How many figure in the media situation, the TV situation? It's only now I can even see black people on TV. And if they come over strong, too 'ethnic', it's either a joke or a threat.

"There's no in between, nothing *good*, in the eyes of those who control things. That's why a young black British man will check for James Brown in the '90s. And that ain't so different anywhere else."

Beresford "Jazzie B" Romeo,
Soul II Soul, 1990

"But a woman makes . . . a better man," sang James Brown in his 1966 R'n'B No 1, "It's A Man's Man's Man's World". Showbiz only, claim most of the women, the soul sisters, who amplified his message down through the years. Not something by which Brown himself lived.

But black Briton Beresford Romeo, better known as Jazzie B, believed those words when he heard them. Four years ago, at the height of London's "rare groove" infatuation, Jazzie was a 22-year-old DJ, who flew out to tour Japan with the briefly re-united JBs. A pirate radio veteran, he also ran a sixteen-person sound system known as Soul II Soul or 'the Funki Dreds'. Five years old, Soul II Soul had been founded by Jazzie and his close friend Philip "Daddae" Harvey. (Its name connects Harvey's reggae "roots" and Jazzie's taste for "chic".) In 1986, Soul II Soul joined with Norman Jay and a white crew, Family Funktion, to throw perhaps the most influential UK warehouse parties of the 1980s. ("Because, at those raves, classes as well as races started to mix.") That same year, they started a regular, weekly club; in 1987 they opened a shop. In 1988, they put out their first two 12" records. Titled "Fairplay" and "Feel Free", the discs were DJ-mixed affairs which revolved around the strong voices of two black British women: Rose Windross and Do'reen Waddell.

In 1989, Soul II Soul released two more records. Both featured the highly individual female singer, Caron Wheeler – and both became international hits. So did an LP, *Club Classics Volume 1* (in America, *Keep On Movin'*), which relaunched the previous Soul II Soul grooves onto a global audience. *Keep On Movin'* sold 1.5 million copies in the US and over a million copies internationally, making it the fastest-selling album in Virgin Records' history. In the autumn of 1989, Soul II Soul opened their second

London shop; six months later, they purchased a site in L.A. Jazzie
B was bestowed with the American NAACP (National Association
for the Advancement of Colored People) Role Model of 1989
Award. And the crew received six American Grammy Award
nominations, two of which they won, in addition to three 1989
Soul Train Awards. The sound system has also given birth to a
black talent agency, an electronics company, a Soul II Soul
Visions film and video consortium, and a Soul II Soul record label
of Romeo's own.

Despite the subsequent double-page ads in *Billboard*, Soul II
Soul were not a phenomenon created by the might of a record
company. Their first UK sales came as a surprise to the Virgin
label, who knew little of London's dance-music marketing scene.
Soul II Soul were built – like James Brown's Revue – from the
street and from an intimate knowledge of what listeners want.
"What has been building up," said Jazzie B in 1988, "is two
Londons. A street scene which now has its own business, its own
public, its own entertainment. And the straight record companies,
still tryin' to sell George Michael."

In the post hip-hop universe of DJ and producer-led hits, Soul
II Soul are a singular fusion: a mixture of James Brown's funky
family with the Caribbean sound-system heritage. Fashion and
visual imagery is important – from the clothes in the Soul II Soul
shops through the Funki Dred banners which festoon their clubs.
And dance too is central; designer-dancer Nummi Olaiya, whose
silhouette appears on the crew's first album, became almost as
much a symbol of Soul II Soul as Jazzie B. Romeo is always careful
to credit his full, multi-racial collective: his co-producer Nellee
Hooper, DJs Solemole HB (Romeo's brother), Jazzy Q, Crime,
Lee and Trevor "Madhatter" Nelson; designer Nicolai Bean;
partners Daddae Harvey and Sparky D; PA Corinna Pyke and fan club

director Paulette Romeo (Jazzie's sister). He even tends to name the staff of each Soul II Soul shop, where records nestle next to designer goods.

Soul II Soul symbolizes a populist, post-modern black aesthetic. One which takes the text of diaspora and funnels it into that same Afro-American call to arms: Express Yourself! ("Cause it's all about expression," sings Rose Windross on Soul II Soul's "Fairplay".) "Nobody can explain just how they feel about it," says Wunmi Olaiya, "but wherever you go in the world, this music can be your bond. Jazzie raps, Caron sings, I dance – and it's all the same, in a way." Music is seen as an apotheosis of both social and individual life: "Elevate your mind, free your soul / Feel the music / Let your body take control," proselytizes Soul II Soul's 1989 "Get A Life". *Soul II Soul Volume II (1990 – A New Decade)* contains a song called "Our Time Has Come". "Because," says Romeo, "all the things that people had to sacrifice way back then can only begin to be understood now."

And one of the most important, in Romeo's own view, is the *female* component of expressive energy. He considers it a primary force – right across the diaspora. "Yeah, and you can put that down in print. Women are the superiors. That doesn't threaten me, that's like a very ancient thing, goin' back towards zero. In fact, if there was a faith I believe in as strongly as I believe in my culture, it would be women. And the reason why is they breed life . . . in the text that they are able to *take care* of the valuable things in life."

That's what you *hear*, claims Jazzie B, in the female voices James Brown managed to find yet was afraid to fully release: Bea Ford, Anna King, Marva Whitney, Lyn Collins, Martha High, Vicki Anderson. "James Brown is the father, he is the symbol of somebody in this business who maintained himself," says Romeo, "and definitely the biggest influence on me, both musically and career-wise. Yet, at the same time, he remains a human being, with personal problems in his life. Things that start from way back – way, way, way, way back. Because carin' and lovin' and affection are necessary to all human beings. You don't have that already in your life – you can't, you just *can't* give."

Soul II Soul took the primacy Jazzie heard from the great women's voices of soul and added to it what he calls the "lessons" taught by James Brown. "Which, for me, is the ties between the race – the ties and the history. You only get someone like Prince because, somewhere along the line, you had someone like James Brown. And only he could do that – you couldn't have had a white artist like Elvis Presley doin' that. You have to see how he turned the negative into the positive; that's where you can learn."

More like Prince than Brown, however, Romeo himself feels free to take the important cues from his female colleagues (and Soul II Soul has many — after Waddell, Windross and Wheeler have come vocalists Victoria Wilson-James, Kym Mazelle, Lamya Al-Mughery and Marcie Lewis). "I have no qualms about that at all," he says firmly. "I'm not sayin' I'm the best guy around or no nonsense like that. It's just that this form of respect and equality is something I'm willing to give. And that changes how you approach your music, your business, even your history."

The rise of Soul II Soul has paralleled a fresh movement of black cultural awareness taking place around the world. This time round it is rooted, not in a sense of cultural difference, but in the confidence of identity forged by those who came before. From the Funki Dred haircut to Bobby Brown's "tramlined" sideburns, from the House of Knowledge in London to Kenté cloth in boutiques across America, from leather "consciousness badges" bearing the image of Mother Africa to back-tilted baseball caps, this movement celebrates cultural democracy – even as it explicitly questions the notion of a sovereign West. Much of this strength, this confidence, says Jazzie B, is still to be found in James Brown. "For people to be usin' his stuff now – that comes direct from him, from whatever gifts he was given. James Brown could have turned around and said 'YEAH! I *am* GOD! Anything black people do, it's all *about me*!' But it wasn't like that. He influenced us for the good, whatever his personal failings."

Jazzie leans forward. "It's like seeing your family tree, when you run all these things down that James Brown made us see. Like: why would you want to have a sound like THAT? Why is hip-hop so raw? Why is soul so emotional? Why come out with R'n'B? Who MADE jazz? *Begin* to answer those things and all of a sudden you see: if all the black people around the world stood up and joined their hands – look how many of us there ARE! This is no 'minority'. Culturally, we are dominant."

Which is, in the end, the message and legacy of Jamesian funk, just as it was and is the message of hip-hop and the secret, spiritual signal of black repetition both "sacred" and "secular". That culture is, and should be, basically anti-apocalyptic. That the real struggle to be takes place outside the battles for representation within the academies and the media. That the authority with which we invest "official" languages, "official" culture and "official" institutions exists to be questioned in proportion to its righteousness.

Afrocentric cultures tell us our choice is not between Jesus, Moses and Mohammed – but between human transcendence and human tragedy, spiritual unity and social exhaustion. And they teach us how many facets of Eurocentric life – from the timeframes which govern our actions through the rules which dictate "proper" speech – are less infallible truths than historical superimpositions.

There are many barriers to Robert Farris Thompson's world where "equal potencies" (and their corollary, global brotherhood) are acknowledged. In the West, our very idea of what constitutes culture has been immunized against wide-ranging, trans-cultural revelation. Our histories are white histories, our geographies white geographies. Our culture is word-dominated, and yet it is word-culture in only the smallest sense: literal and skeletal rather than richly resonant and allusive. When the great tone-languages of China and Africa fall outside our definition of "the classics", it is no surprise we fail to grasp jazz and gospel singing as sacraments.

Eurocentric pundits dismiss hip-hop *bricolage* as aural bric-à-brac. To them it is a novelty, a "subculture" – just as James Brown's cape routine has been perceived as a novelty *act.* To such chilly intellects, culture as a profound and dynamic force – a communication above and beyond politics – is a threatening proposition.

After all, it calls into question the established distribution of power. It calls to account the expertise of anointed commentators. And it disciplines us severely – with an insistence on constant open-mindedness. The sort of unprejudiced enquiry Louis Dupré characterizes as "an obedient attention to possible messages, a waiting in expectation . . . far beyond ordinary open-mindedness, the spiritual man of the present must be willing to suspend even unquestionable assumptions."

In the Western world, for decades now, modernist doubt has held the ticket to accepted "modern" standing as art. And now black kids in tennis shoes are going to rock the boat? Well, the answer is YES. It doesn't mean the West will change its priorities tomorrow. But what it does mean is this – that those tennis shoes themselves signify something which transcends semiotics, just as James Brown's groove is but a pass-key to the riches of a whole world diaspora. And warnings not to "mix things up" now sport the vested interest once inherent in staying "separate but equal".

"As a black artist I'd like to say something," that genial giant of crossover Louis Jordan told Arnold Shaw, two years before he died. "There is nothing that the white artist has invented or come along with in the form of jazz or entertainment . . . He hasn't invented anything. Rock 'n' roll was not a marriage of rhythm and blues or country and Western. That's white publicity. Rock 'n' roll was just a white imitation, a white adaptation of Negro rhythm and blues.

"What the white artist has done," said Jordan, "and they started it fifteen or twenty years ago, was they started that publicity and eliminating talk of the black artist. They eliminated talking about who did what and how good it was, and they started talking about white artists."

Any contemporary black artist of consequence – visual, literary or musical – would readily acknowledge Jordan's point about pervasive "white publicity". Yet the very reticence of black cultures has also endowed them with strength. Despite three centuries of effort, three centuries of concerted Caucasian publicity, the black contribution to our common world is daily made more evident. The Eurocentric hegemony is shifting and Babylon may not fall, but cultural debate must change. After all, he who will not deal in the real vocabulary of his age is doomed to live in its margins. And what an age we are facing now! "The

'90s," chuckles Robert Farris Thompson, "are gonna be like synthesis time at the ol' ranch. Can you even imagine what the Paris and the London and the New York of the '90s will *be*? What the Romans didn't realize when they built those wonderful roads is that Onward Christian Soldiers would someday mean an Afrocentric world spreading its might through all those channels.

"The opening up of Europe to itself," he adds, "will also mean the opening up of black Paris to all of France, of black London to all of Europe. From Warsaw to Edinburgh, you're gonna get some very funky things going on."

So jump back, Cadillac. And prepare for the kind of prolific, right-now creativity the Godfather pioneered. James Brown offered black people everywhere the self-image of respect, of continuity and meaningful tradition. His ritual, his capes and theatrics were not about beckoning destiny as much as about things already accomplished. James said: *You are HERE*! He looked at life not with fear, but for constant, spiritual affirmation. In July of 1989, Jesse Jackson spoke to the senior class of Washington DC's black Dunbar High School. To a thunderous, standing ovation, the black politician told them, "We can rule not only ourselves, but we can rule the world."

And that is the tune James Brown has been dancing to, for almost forty years.

index

Quincy Jones   150, 152
Nathaniel Jones   52
Louis Jordan   33, 36, 45-6, 50,
    76-8, 81-2, 87, 117, 173
Tom Joyner   83, 98-101, 108,
    133

Lawrence Kasdan   132
KC and the Sunshine
    Band   105
Charles Keil   73, 87
Alphonso "Country"
    Kellum   29, 56
Nat Kendrick   42
Anna King   169
Martin Luther King   23, 44, 55,
    65-7, 124
Fela Kuti   92

Max L-X   149
Major Lance   41
John Landis   130-1, 133
Amanda Lear   104
Spike Lee   154
Barry Levison   132

Gordon Mac   159
Kristine McKenna   16
Madonna   150
Elsie "TV" Mae   29

Pigmeat Markham   123
Branford Marsalis   146
Dave Marsh   41
Calvin Marshall   125
Hearlon "Sharp Cheese"
    Martin   29
August Meier   50
Melle Mell   137, 150-1,
    153
James Meredith   55
George Michael   168
Claudia Mitchell-Kernan   36
Melba Moore   104
Giorgio Moroder   103
Van Morrison   51
John Morthland   132
Alison Moyet   134
Eddie Murphy   37
Salim Muwakkil   110

Syd Nathan   35, 42, 103, 120
Hal Neely   103
Marco Nelson   159
Trevor "Madhatter"
    Nelson   161, 168
Huey Newton   45
Richard Milhouse Nixon   94
Jimmy "Chank" Nolen   29, 56,
    134
Robert Nunnally   101

David Toop

THE RAP ATTACK
African Jive to New York Hip Hop

The Rap Attack, the first book on rap, remains the definitive book on the subject. Rap first emerged in New York's Harlem and Bronx, and quickly spread to all corners of the globe. Rap artists are now a regular feature of musical and counter-cultural life in all major cities, and the influence of rap itself is to be found in all contemporary popular music. In the words of Charlie Gillet, read the *The Rap Attack* and "discover the pioneers of the most potent new sound of the eighties."

"The most authoritative book yet on the New York street phenomenon." *Record Mirror*

"A coherently written and well researched introduction to a fascinating musically-based culture."
Next

172 pages/illustrated/£4.95

Simon Reynolds

BLISSED OUT
The Raptures of Rock

Blissed Out is a celebration of the "underground" music of today. From hardcore to hip hop, acid rock to acid house, these cults contradict the widely-held view that "rock is dead" and that there is nothing left for musicians to do but play pick'n'mix with thirty years of pop history. When he writes about his favourite bands, Throwing Muses, My Bloody Valentine, The Young Gods, Loop, Simon Reynolds captures the giddy exhilaration of their music.

192 pages/£8.99

Ian Breakwell & Paul Hammond (eds)

SEEING IN THE DARK
A Compendium of Cinemagoing

"It was a former skating rink, a long narrow building with the screen in the middle, because projectors in 1916 didn't have the throw. The admission was two jamjars and one jamjar. For two you got a proper seat. For one you sat *behind* the screen to watch the silent film, using a hand mirror to read the intertitles." (Denis Norden)

"The manager was patrolling the aisles and found a pair of lady's panties on the floor by the back stalls. He picked them up and courteously enquired of the young woman sitting closest with her boyfriend if they were hers. With equal decorum she replied, 'Oh no, mine are in my handbag.'" (Noel Spence)

For a generation of cinemagoers, food was sweet popcorn, sex began in double seats and post-modernism was reels played in the wrong order. The hundred contributors to *Seeing in the Dark* illuminate the picture palace with a bizarre, funny collection of movie tales. Contributors include: Angus Calder, Kevin Coyne, Ivor Cutler, Janice Eidus, Nicole Ward Jouve, James Kelman, Deborah Moggach, Daniel Moyano, Tom Raworth, Carolee Schneeman, Lynne Tillman, David Toop and Haifa Zangana.

176 pages/£10.99/illustrated

Elfriede Jelinek

THE PIANO TEACHER

"Good books, like haircuts, should fill you with awe, change your life, or make you long for another. Elfriede Jelinek's *The Piano Teacher* manages to fulfil at least two of these demands in a reckless recital that is difficult to read and difficult to stop reading. The racy, relentless, consuming style is a metaphor for passion: impossible to ignore."
Carole Morin, *New Statesmen & Society*

"Something of a land-mine . . . a brilliant, deadly book."
Elizabeth J. Young, *City Limits*

"Some may see, in the pain of this novel, its panic and its deep despair, a model of current writing. For others, *The Piano Teacher* will remain a perverse horror story of a mother's love taken to its logical, deadly extreme."
Angela McRobbie, *The Independent*

288 pages/£7.95

Oscar Hijuelos

OUR HOUSE IN THE LAST WORLD

by the author of the internationally-acclaimed *The Mambo Kings Play Songs of Love*

"A first novel about an urban family in New York City, told in an oblique, lyric voice, with an air of absolute authenticity and assurance."
Joyce Carol Oates

"There is more than a touch of satire in Mr Hijuelos's writing, but he never loses the syntax of magic . . . a loving and deeply felt tribute."
New York Times

"Sometimes brilliant, this first novel from Cuban New Yorker Hijuelos has a terrible raging power that lifts it clear of the usual sociological categories that semi-autobiographical writing gets consigned to, and manages to hit that Nelson Algren note in which people's failure in life becomes their personal poetry. I loved it."
Time Out

"An intoxicating first novel, a mesmeric voyage through eight decades of a family's life."
The Voice

240 pages/£6.95

also published by serpent's tail

Raul Nuñez

THE LONELY HEARTS CLUB

"The singles scene of Barcelona's lonely low life. Sweet and seedy."
Elle

"A celebration of the wit and squalor of Barcelona's mean streets."
City Limits

"This tough and funny story of low life in Barcelona manages to convey the immense charm of that city without once mentioning Gaudi . . . A story of striking freshness, all the fresher for being so casually conveyed."
The Independent

"A sardonic view of human relations . . ."
The Guardian

"Threatens to do for Barcelona what *No Mean City* once did for Glasgow."
Glasgow Herald

"A funny low life novel of Barcelona."
The Times

160 pages/£6.95

Marsha Rowe (ed)

SEX AND THE CITY

"Unerringly entertaining and thought provoking"
Joanna Briscoe, *Girl About Town*

"The whole book comes into the category of good dirty fun, and is not the worse for that."
Robert Nye, *The Guardian*

"A mixture of 1980's eroticism, sexual humiliation and an underlying wistful longing for the milk of human kindness, seemingly destroyed by urban living. Compulsive stuff."
The List

"Strangely intriguing."
Glasgow Herald

"There is no other collection quite like *Sex and the City*." *TES*

240 pages/£5.95